Microsoft® Office 2010

Prentice Hall
is an imprint of

PEARSON

Harlow, England • London • New York • Boston ...   ...ngapore • Hong Kong
Tokyo • Seoul • Taipei • New Delhi • Cape Town • ...   ...Munich • Paris • Milan

PEARSON EDUCATION LIMITED

Edinburgh Gate
Harlow CM20 2JE
Tel: +44 (0)1279 623623
Fax: +44 (0)1279 431059
Website: www.pearsoned.co.uk

First published in Great Britain in 2010

Pearson Education is not responsible for the content of third party internet sites.

ISBN: 978-0-273-73612-7

British Library Cataloguing-in-Publication Data
A catalogue record for this book is available from the British Library

Library of Congress Cataloging-in-Publication Data
Holden, Greg.
  Microsoft Office 2010 in simple steps / Greg Holden.
      p. cm.
  ISBN 978-0-273-73612-7 (pbk.)
  1. Microsoft Office. 2. Business--Computer programs. I. Title.
  HF5548.4.M525H6468 2010
  005.5--dc22
                            2010022307

Microsoft screen shots reprinted with permission from Microsoft Corporation.

10 9 8 7 6 5 4 3 2 1
14 13 12 11 10

Designed by pentacorbig, High Wycombe
Typeset in 11/14 pt ITC Stone Sans by 30
Printed and bound in Great Britain by Scotprint, Edinburgh

Microsoft®

Office
2010

in **Simple**
steps

Greg Holden

Use your computer with confidence

Get to grips with practical computing tasks with minimal time, fuss and bother.

In Simple Steps guides guarantee immediate results. They tell you everything you need to know on a specific application; from the most essential tasks to master, to every activity you'll want to accomplish, through to solving the most common problems you'll encounter.

Helpful features

To build your confidence and help you to get the most out of your computer, practical hints, tips and shortcuts feature on every page:

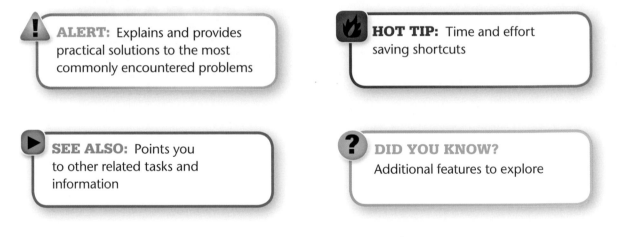

ALERT: Explains and provides practical solutions to the most commonly encountered problems

HOT TIP: Time and effort saving shortcuts

SEE ALSO: Points you to other related tasks and information

DID YOU KNOW? Additional features to explore

WHAT DOES THIS MEAN? Jargon and technical terms explained in plain English

Practical. Simple. Fast.

in **Simple** steps

Dedication:

To Peggy and our bright future together.

Author's acknowledgements:

Two teams help put together the *Simple Steps* books I've written. At home, I want to acknowledge the help of my assistant, Ann Lindner, and my collaborator, Patti Short. In the UK, thanks to Steve Temblett, Katy Robinson and the rest of the Pearson staff for their help and support.

Contents at a glance

9 Getting organised with Outlook

Top 10 Office 2010 Problems Solved

Contents

2 Working with text

3 Working with art and photos

4 Applying themes and formatting

5 Creating a Word document

6 Working with Excel spreadsheets

7 Assembling PowerPoint presentations

8 Creating an Access database

9 Getting organised with Outlook

Top 10 Office 2010 Problems Solved

Top 10 Office 2010 Tips

Tip 1: Launch an Office application

If you've used Windows before, you probably know the place to start any application is the Start button on the taskbar. By default, the Start button is in the lower left-hand corner of your desktop, though you can drag the desktop to other sides if you wish. Windows 7 gives you several options for finding Office applications among your installed programs:

1 Click the Start button.

2 Click All Programs.

3 Click Microsoft Office.

4 Click Microsoft Office Tools to access a new feature: a submenu full of options, such as Microsoft Clip Organizer (for adding clip art images to documents), Microsoft Office Picture Manager (for locating, editing, renaming or emailing images) and more.

5 Click the application you want to open.

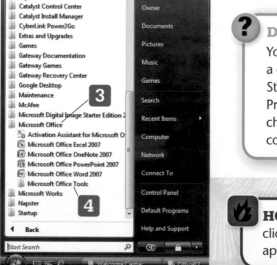

? DID YOU KNOW?

You can start any Office application by creating a desktop shortcut for it or by 'pinning' it to the Start menu. Right-click the application's icon (in Program Files\Microsoft Office\Office2010) and choose Pin to Start Menu or Shortcut from the context menu.

🔥 HOT TIP: If you used the application recently, click the Start button. The application's name will appear in the Start menu.

⚠ ALERT: Don't type 'Microsoft' as the program name. You'll end up with a long list of applications. Simply type 'Word', 'Excel' and so on.

Tip 2: Edit text

Once you have learned to select the text you want (see Chapter 2), you can edit the text so it looks and reads the way you want. Most of the time, that means you'll want to cut, copy or paste text from one location to another. You can use keyboard commands for any of those functions; however, you can also use drag-and-drop to copy or move text from one file to another, or from one location to another in the same file.

1 Use one of the techniques described in Select text in Chapter 2, or drag the text cursor over your chosen text to select it. The text is highlighted in black to indicate that it has been selected.

2 Do one of the following:

- Type your new text to immediately replace the highlighted text.

- Press Backspace or Delete (Del) to delete the text and then type the new text.

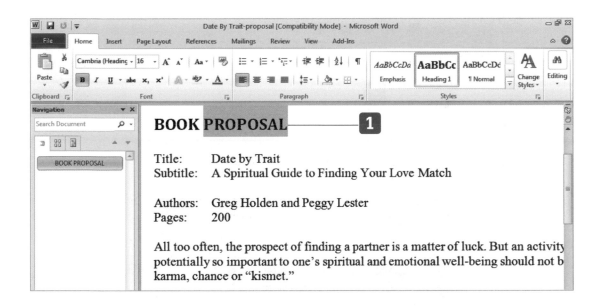

? DID YOU KNOW?

You can double-click a word to select it or triple-click a paragraph to select it.

Tip 3: Place a picture

Whether you have chosen an image from Office's Clip Art libraries or use a photo taken with your digital camera, you can easily add the image to a document. You can add a file from a CD-ROM, directly from your digital camera, from a 'flash' USB drive, or from a file on your hard disk. Before you add an image you can view a thumbnail to make sure it's the one you want.

1 Click the Insert tab.

2 Click Picture.

3 Click one of your Favorite Links or the drop-down list arrow to locate an image.

4 Click an image file.

5 Click Insert.

? **DID YOU KNOW?**

You can link to a file as well as insert it by clicking the drop-down list arrow next to Insert and choosing Link to File.

Tip 4: Apply a theme

Office makes two kinds of design themes available to you: predesigned themes that come ready to use and custom themes that you can create yourself. Each theme contains a palette of 12 complementary colours as well as preselected fonts and other special effects. You don't see the colours all at once; some are accent colours used for elements like drop shadows or hyperlinks. You can view and change any of the colours if you want to match certain colours you use in your other publications.

1 Open the file to which you want to apply a theme.

2 Click either the Page Layout or Design tab.

3 Click the Themes button to display the gallery of available themes.

4 Click your chosen theme to apply its fonts and colours to the current document.

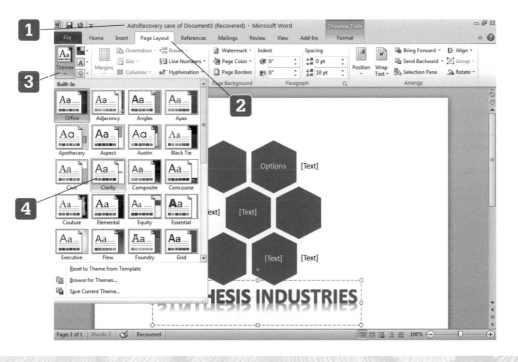

Tip 5: Create an outline

An outline is a hierarchical way of organising a set of information into categories and subcategories. You can either create an outline from scratch while in Outline view, or you can convert the items in a bulleted or numbered list into an outline. These steps get you started on creating an outline from scratch.

1 Open a new file, and click the Page Layout tab.

2 Click the Outline View button.

3 Type a heading for your outline, and press Enter.

4 If you need to change the heading level to a higher or lower one, position the insertion point at the beginning of the heading and click the Promote or Demote buttons.

5 Move to the next line and type a subheading or item in the outline. Click the Promote or Demote buttons to change the level as needed.

6 When you're done, click Close Outline View.

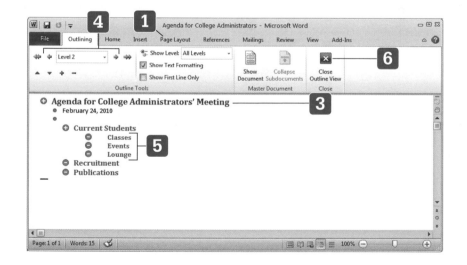

? DID YOU KNOW?

You can also position the cursor anywhere in a heading and click the Move Up or Move Down buttons until it is positioned correctly in the outline.

Tip 6: Enter Excel worksheet values

Entering values in worksheet cells is one of the basic tasks associated with spreadsheets. Values can take the form of whole numbers, decimals, percentages or dates. You can enter numeric values either by using the number keys at the top of your keyboard or by pressing the Num Lock key.

1 Click the cell where you want to enter a value.

2 Type the value.

3 Press Enter.

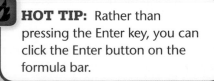

Microsoft Excel screenshot showing the table:

	A	B	C	D	E	F	G	H	I	J
41	36	120,288	65,041	16	24	40	7,334.75			
42	37	120,279	47,169	19	7	26	6,277.90			
43	38	120,284	49,174	73	45	118	1,644.80			
44	39	120,298	46,640	4,384	54	4,439	27.44			
45	40	120,279	53,343	440	605	1,045	273.39			
46	41	120,289	50,301	59	10	69	2,037.21			
47	42	120,300	54,405	1,142	318	1,461	105.33			
48	43	120,256	65,667	11	3	15	10,517.18			
49	44	120,283	43,262	102	3	105	1,178.70			
50	45	120,360	45,808	236	5	241	510.04			
51	46	120,267	56,476	19	6	25	6,435.91			
52	47	120,302	43,689	87	2	89	1,375.62			
53	48	120,294	54,101	35	10	44	3,459.98			
54	49	120,467	51,285	49	10	59	2,471.36			
55	Grand Total	5,894,141	2,451,081	66,544	4,756	71,300	88.58			
56										
57										

Cell F46 = 69.061135418388. File name: LegDensity02_C [Last saved by user]. Ready. 100%

HOT TIP: Rather than pressing the Enter key, you can click the Enter button on the formula bar.

DID YOU KNOW?
When you begin to enter a date or time, Excel recognises the entries (if they correspond to one of its built-in date or time formats) and changes the information to fit its default date or time format.

Tip 7: Create a PowerPoint presentation

If you don't want to create a presentation from scratch (see Chapter 7), turn to the templates that Office 2010 provides you. PowerPoint comes with a selection of installed templates. If you don't find the one you want, you'll find a wide selection at Microsoft Office Online. You can choose everything from invitations to agendas. By starting with a template, you get a suggested set of slides that you can modify to fit your own needs.

1 Click the File tab.

2 Click New.

3 Click one of the options in the categories of templates that either came with PowerPoint or that you can access at Office Online.

4 Select the template you want.

5 Click Create.

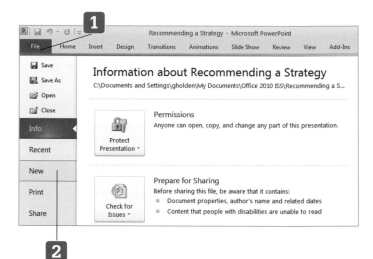

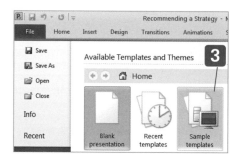

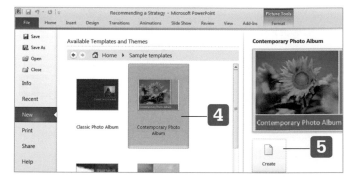

? DID YOU KNOW?

To download the Microsoft Office Online templates, you need to use Internet Explorer rather than another browser; an Active X control may have to be installed so you can view and install the template you want.

Tip 8: Manage Access database objects

The objects that make up a database are there to help you track and work with your data. But you don't have to stick with the default names of these objects. You can create new objects, hide some objects or delete them. That way, each database will only have the selection of objects you need.

1 Double-click an object in the navigation pane to open it, or right-click the object to change its design.

2 Choose Delete from the context menu to delete the object.

3 Click the Create tab.

4 Click the button for the type of object you want to create.

5 Work with the object when it opens in the reading pane.

6 Click the object's Close button when you are finished.

Tip 9: Add a new contact

Contacts are one of the fundamental pieces of information you can track and work with in Outlook. A contact is a person or business you need to communicate with, either by phone, fax, IM, text or email. Outlook can help you with all of these media: it gives you a way to store names, addresses and contact information as well as other essential information about each contact such as birthdays, account information, company names or titles.

1 Click the Contacts view button in the navigation pane.

2 Click New Contact.

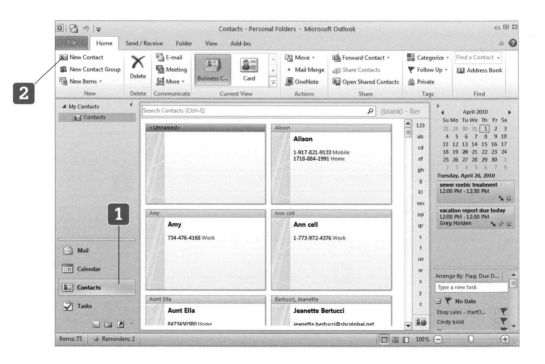

? DID YOU KNOW?

In the process of creating a contact, you also create an electronic business card, which you can share with others as an email attachment.

3 When the Contact window opens, fill in the contact information. The Contact window contains its own set of ribbon tabs: Contact, Insert, Format Text and Review.

4 When you enter a phone number, fill in your current location in the Location Information dialogue box and then click OK.

5 Click Details on the Contact tab and fill in more detailed information about the contact.

6 Click the Save & Close button on the Contact tab.

HOT TIP: Double-click anywhere in the reading pane to create a new contact.

Tip 10: Send an email message

When you have typed the text of your email message and have attached files and signatures as needed, you can send it. You can send and receive messages at the same time, and control the way Outlook sends messages as well. When you send a message, Outlook moves it to the Outbox folder, where it stays while Outlook connects to your email server and sends the mail.

1 Create your message.

2 Click the Send button to send the file.

3 To change the way Outlook sends and receives email, click the Options tab and then cick More Options.

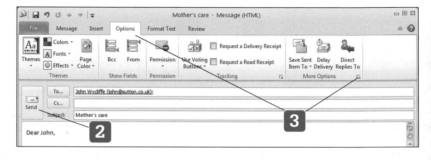

4 Click the down arrow next to Importance and choose the level of importance for the message.

5 Click here to have a delivery receipt sent to yourself.

6 Check this box and enter a time to schedule later delivery of the message.

7 Click OK.

? DID YOU KNOW?

To insert a miniature version of your calendar in an email message, click the Insert tab at the top of the message window and then click the Calendar button.

1 Getting acquainted with Office 2010

Introduction

Congratulations on choosing Microsoft Office 2010 as your productivity and information management tool. You'll be happy to discover that Office 2010's suite of programs provide you with everything you need to manage data, text and presentations, and to communicate with anyone online. Each of the programs – Word, Excel, Access, PowerPoint, Outlook and Publisher – is designed to perform specialised tasks. But they are closely integrated with one another and with the Web as well.

If you have used previous versions of Office, you'll find a few surprises. If you are upgrading from Office 2007 to 2010, the differences are significant but not dramatic. For instance, you'll notice right away that the Start menu is gone, and in its place near the top left-hand corner of the top of the application window is the familiar File menu. The options for sharing, printing and converting documents are more streamlined and visually oriented than previously. If you are upgrading from Office 2003 or an earlier version, you'll immediately notice that the area at the top of the application window is more complex and feature-rich than ever before (it's called the ribbon). Don't worry; none of your favourite menu commands or functions is missing. They've just been moved around so you can find them more easily. Once you've acquainted yourself with the new interface and features, you'll find that Office 2010 is easier to use, faster and more reliable than previous versions.

If this is your first time using Office, you'll find each program's learning curve especially easy to climb. That's due in part to the suite's intuitive nature, and in part to visual aids such as ScreenTips, task panes, an improved status bar, and extensive Help options. You don't need to be a computer guru to get up and running with Office. In this first chapter you'll learn everything you need to know to start working with any of the Office 2010 applications.

It is important to note that Office 2010 comes in several editions and computer manufacturers often add their own touches. As a result, your screen may not look exactly like what you'll see in the screenshots in this book (but it'll be close).

Tour Office 2010's new features

Office 2010 looks very much like its predecessor, Office 2007, but with a few noticeable differences. Taking a moment to explore some of those differences will help you take advantage of the new features available. They will help you share, print and back up your files easier than ever before.

1 Click the File tab to bring it to the front.

2 Click Convert to view options for saving your file in a different format, if needed.

3 Click Protect Document to quickly change sharing permissions for the file.

4 If you lose data due to a computer problem, scan these previous versions automatically saved by Word and choose one to recover your work.

5 Click Share.

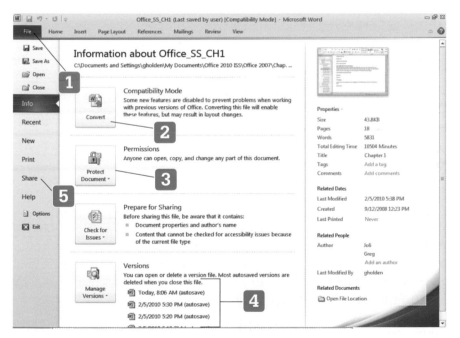

HOT TIP: The Recent option on the File tab displays a list of files you've worked on recently, so you can work with them again if needed.

6 Click Save to SkyDrive.

7 Read about this new feature for backing your files up on a remote server, which you'll explore later.

8 Click here to publish the file as a blog post.

9 Click Home.

10 Copy some text, then paste it by pressing Ctrl+V (the Ctrl and V keys together). Click the Paste Options menu to see the options there.

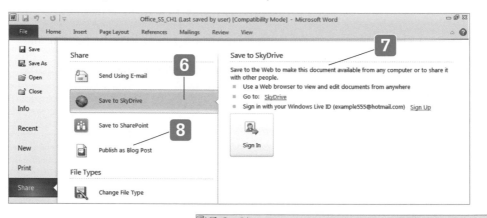

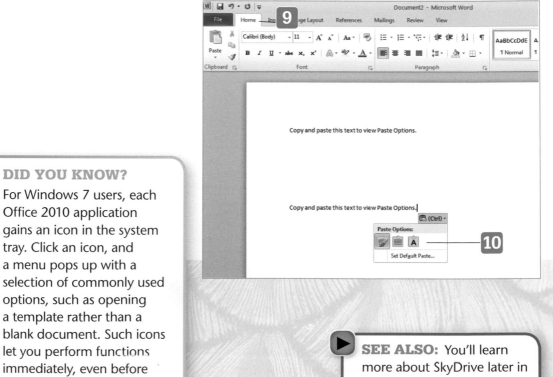

DID YOU KNOW?

For Windows 7 users, each Office 2010 application gains an icon in the system tray. Click an icon, and a menu pops up with a selection of commonly used options, such as opening a template rather than a blank document. Such icons let you perform functions immediately, even before you open the application.

SEE ALSO: You'll learn more about SkyDrive later in this chapter.

Launch an Office application

If you've used Windows before, you probably know the place to start any application is the Start button on the taskbar. By default, the Start button is in the lower left-hand corner of your desktop, though you can drag the desktop to other sides if you wish. Windows 7 gives you several options for finding Office applications among your installed programs.

1 Click the Start button.

2 Click All Programs.

3 Click Microsoft Office.

4 Click Microsoft Office Tools to access a new feature: a submenu full of options such as Microsoft Clip Organizer (for adding clip art images to documents), Microsoft Office Picture Manager (for locating, editing, renaming or emailing images) and more.

5 Click the application you want to open.

DID YOU KNOW?

You can start any Office application by creating a desktop shortcut for it or by 'pinning' it to the Start menu. Right-click the application's icon (in Program Files\Microsoft Office\Office2010) and choose Pin to Start Menu or Shortcut from the context menu.

HOT TIP: If you used the application recently, click the Start button. The application's name will appear in the Start menu.

ALERT: Don't type 'Microsoft' as the program name. You'll end up with a long list of applications. Simply type 'Word', 'Excel', and so on.

Work with the Office program window

Once you open an Office application, the program window opens. The specifics vary from one program to another. But if you learn some of the common features then you'll be able to use the program more easily. These include the File tab with its 'backstage view' of the current file and application you're using; the quick access toolbar; the status bar; the ribbon; the System Tray icons; and the Zoom controls. They are common to all of the Office applications and some are new to Office 2010. Some, like the main program window, will have to be discovered as you work with the application. You can click on many of the main features to learn what they do.

1 File tab: as described earlier in this chapter, the File tab contains general controls for printing, sharing, permissions and other settings.

2 Quick access toolbar: click to perform common functions such as Save, Undo and Redo; customise the toolbar to add more commands.

3 Ribbon: click tools and choose commands grouped by category in different tabs.

4 Program window: work with presentations, data, text or other content here.

5 Zoom controls: all Office applications let you zoom in or out using slider or buttons.

6 View buttons: click to switch between views.

7 Status bar: shows details about current document.

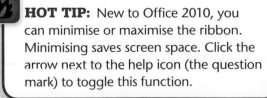

HOT TIP: New to Office 2010, you can minimise or maximise the ribbon. Minimising saves screen space. Click the arrow next to the help icon (the question mark) to toggle this function.

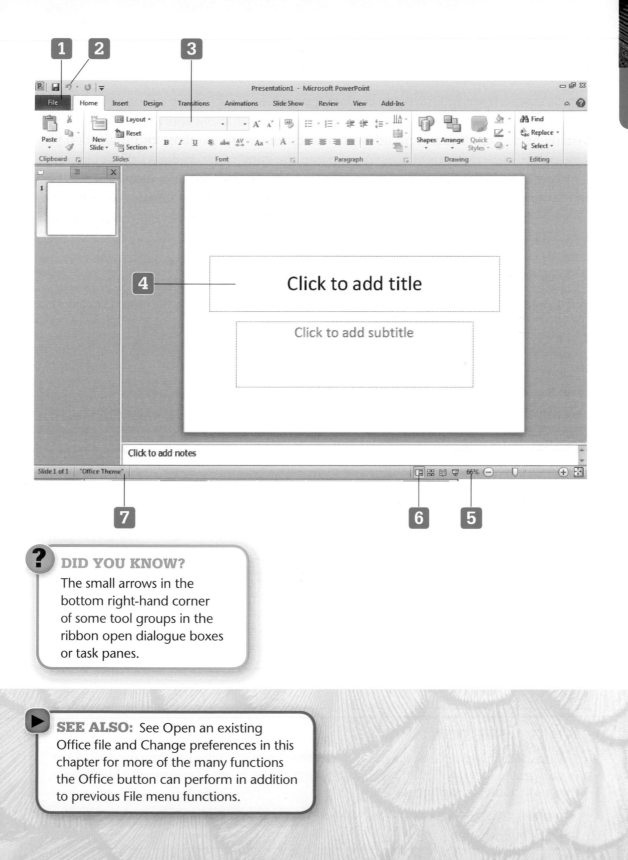

▶ SEE ALSO: See Open an existing Office file and Change preferences in this chapter for more of the many functions the Office button can perform in addition to previous File menu functions.

Open an Office file

If you are launching an Office application, a new blank document opens automatically so you can start working with it. If you already have the application open, you can open as many new presentation, spreadsheet, word processing, database or publication files as you wish. Each document is assigned a generic name such as Book1 or Document1; you need to save the file with a more specific name so you can find it easily. If you click the File tab, you can either choose Open to locate the file or choose the file from a list of recent documents. If you double-click the file's icon, you can launch the application as well if it is not already open.

1 Click the File tab.

2 Click New.

3 Leave the default option, Blank document, selected in the Available Templates. A preview of this or any other new file you choose appears in the task pane on the right-hand side of this window.

4 Click Create. A new blank file appears in the current Office application window.

HOT TIP: You can save time by pressing Ctrl+N instead of clicking the Office button and choosing New. Pressing Ctrl+N causes a new blank file to appear instantly.

WHAT DOES THIS MEAN?

Task pane: a miniature window that opens within the main Office program window. A task pane often has a scroll bar and other controls and can be widened or narrowed by dragging the inside border to the right or left.

Template: a preconfigured document that serves as a shortcut so you don't have to create the file from scratch.

5 To open an existing Office file, click File.

6 Click Open.

7 Choose an option from the Files of type list if you want to choose from files of a certain type.

8 Click the file you want and then click Open. Or, if you want to control exactly how the file is opened, choose one of the available options by clicking the down arrow next to Open:

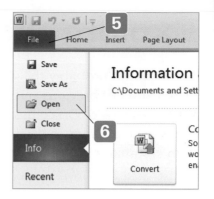

- Open Read-Only opens the file so it can't be edited.

- Open as Copy opens a copy of the file, not the original.

- Open in Browser opens the Web file in a Web browser.

- Open with Transform allows you to transform the file to another format (only works when you try to open an XML file).

- Open and Repair allows you to open a damaged file.

HOT TIP: Press Ctrl+O to display the Open box without having to press the File tab.

? DID YOU KNOW?

If you worked recently on the file you want to open, chances are it will be listed with other recent files when you click the Office button. Click the file's name to open it.

HOT TIP: You can also open a file and launch an Office application simultaneously if you double-click the file's icon in the Computer window, the Documents list or in Windows Explorer.

Explore the ribbon

The ribbon is probably the single most noticeable change in Office 2010 compared with Office 2003 or previous versions. It replaces the system of menus and toolbars these earlier versions of Office used. The ribbon is always located at the top of the Office window. The ribbon is divided into tabs, and each tab contains multiple groups of tools. Each command button in a tool group performs a specific function.

1 Click each of the tabs in turn to display their contents. For instance, open Word and click the Insert tab.

2 Click Table to see the drop-down options beneath it.

3 Drag your mouse down and to the right to draw a table in the current program window.

4 To display a contextual tab (a tab that only appears when needed based upon what you're doing), click SmartArt.

HOT TIP: If you need more screen space, you can minimise the ribbon by double-clicking the tab that is currently in front. Or click the list arrow on the right of the quick access toolbar and choose Minimize the Ribbon.

5 Click one of the SmartArt options.

6 Click OK.

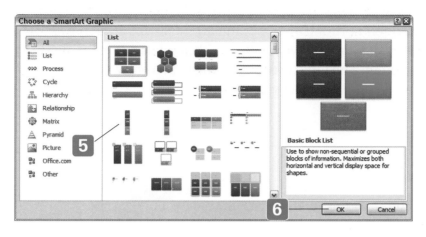

7 Click one of the SmartArt objects you just added. The Design and Format contextual tabs appear.

8 Choose one of the new options that come with the contextual tabs to change the colours or other attributes of the artwork.

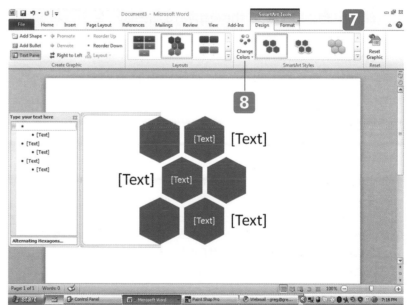

? DID YOU KNOW?

If you want to use keyboard shortcuts instead of ribbon commands, press the Alt or F10 key. KeyTips will appear over each feature in the current view. To hide the KeyTips, press the Alt or F10 key again.

Choose menu commands

Office 2010 has done away with the original series of menus (File, Edit, Format, Tools, and so on) arranged horizontally across the top of an application window. Instead, you'll find menus that drop down when you click the File tab, the quick access toolbar and the mini-toolbar. The same menus you may have grown used to are all there; you just have to look in different places to find them.

Use the File tab

1 Click the File tab.

2 Click the command of your choice.

3 If you see a right arrow next to the menu command, point to the arrow to display a submenu with further options, and choose the one you want.

Use a shortcut menu

4 Right click a cell in a spreadsheet, a paragraph or an image.

5 Choose a command from the shortcut menu.

6 If you see an arrow next to the context menu command, point to the arrow and choose the more specific command on the submenu that appears.

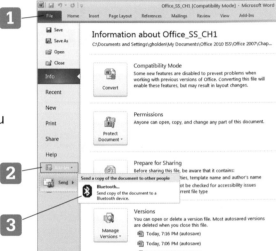

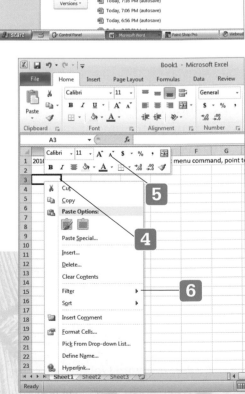

HOT TIP: You can also open a shortcut menu by right-clicking a cell or icon in the program you're working with.

WHAT DOES THIS MEAN?

Mini-toolbar: a small toolbar that appears above selected text.

Work with toolbars

Office 2010, like previous versions, lets you choose toolbar buttons and other commands. Some of the most common commands, including Save and Undo, are found on the quick access toolbar. The quick access toolbar is the most obvious of Office 2010's toolbars; it is always found at the top of the current application window, unless you have customised its settings. Other toolbars are found on the ribbon and act just as those in previous versions of Office.

Choose a toolbar or ribbon command

1 Pass your mouse over a toolbar button to display a ScreenTip explaining what it does.

2 Click the button to execute the command – or click the drop-down arrow next to the button and choose a command or option.

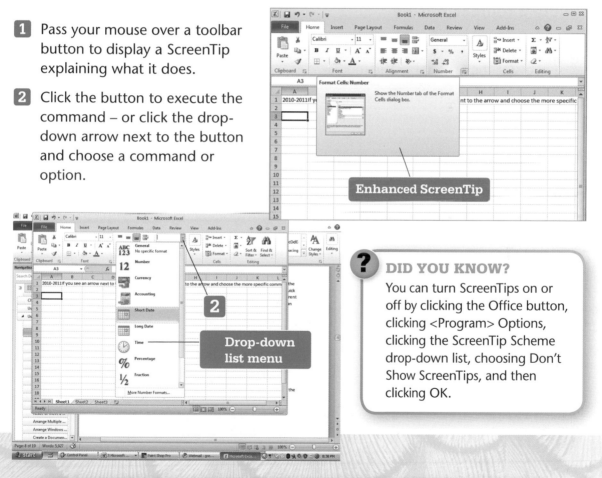

Enhanced ScreenTip

Drop-down list menu

? DID YOU KNOW?

You can turn ScreenTips on or off by clicking the Office button, clicking <Program> Options, clicking the ScreenTip Scheme drop-down list, choosing Don't Show ScreenTips, and then clicking OK.

? DID YOU KNOW?

ScreenTips come in two versions: Enhanced ScreenTips include keyboard commands or graphics. Regular ones take up less space. Click the Office button, click <Program> Options, click the ScreenTip Scheme drop-down list, close Don't Show Enhanced ScreenTips, and click OK to change to regular format.

Manage the quick access toolbar

The quick access toolbar is worth exploring in detail because it allows you to make your most frequently chosen command buttons or groups readily available. Those commands can be ones that are normally hard to find, or that at least take several mouse clicks to execute. You can also move the toolbar below or above the ribbon so you can find it more easily.

Delete a toolbar button

1 Click the Customize Quick Access Toolbar down arrow at the far right of the toolbar.

2 Click one of the ticked items on the drop-down list (ticked items are shown on the toolbar).

Add a toolbar button

Do one of the following:

3 Right-click the command you want to add and choose Add to Quick Access Toolbar. Click the Customize Quick Access Toolbar drop-down list arrow.

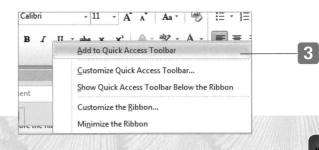

HOT TIP: You can move the quick access toolbar by clicking the Customize Quick Access Toolbar down arrow, then choosing Show Below the Ribbon or Show Above the Ribbon.

4 If you don't see the command you want to add, click the Customize Quick Access Toolbar down arrow and choose More Commands.

5 Click the command you want to add.

6 Click Add.

7 When you are finished adding commands, click OK.

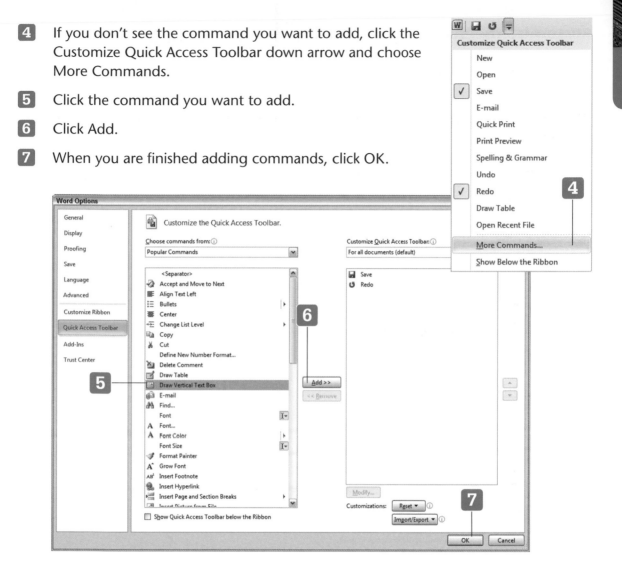

Customise the quick access toolbar

8 Click the Choose commands from list arrow, and choose Popular Commands, All Commands, or pick commands from a specific ribbon.

9 Choose For all documents if you want the commands to be available on the quick access toolbar for all documents/spreadsheets/presentations you create with your Office program of choice. Choose for <document name> if you want the command to available only in the current document.

10 Click the Move Up or Move Down arrows to change the order of buttons.

11 Click OK.

HOT TIP: You can separate each button by clicking <Separator> and then clicking Add. This places a line between buttons.

Choose dialogue box options

Dialogue boxes are indispensible parts of every Office application. They present you with specific options and commands for many functions – sizes of fonts, table formats, and much more. The level of organisation in the ribbon means that some dialogue boxes are accessed differently than in previous versions of Office. But Office 2010's enhanced ScreenTips let you know when a dialogue box is available and even gives you a preview of what it looks like.

1 To display the ScreenTip, pass your mouse pointer over the arrow that points down and to the right if you see one at the bottom of a tool group in the ribbon.

2 Click the button to open the dialogue box.

3 If the dialogue box is divided into separate tabs, click the one that contains the controls you want.

4 Choose the commands you want.

5 Click OK.

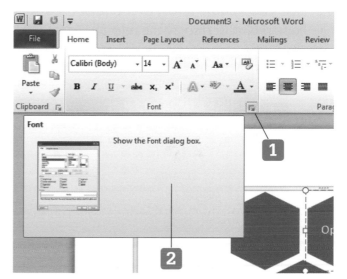

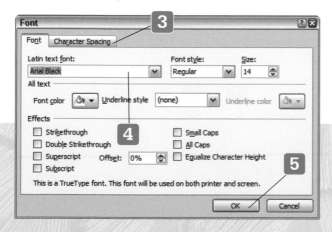

HOT TIP: Many dialogue boxes contain a preview area that lets you see how text or other elements will be formatted based on your selections.

HOT TIP: Press the Tab key to move from one field to another in a dialogue box, instead of having to use your mouse or touchpad to move around. Press Shift+Tab to move backward.

Use the status bar

The status bar is the area at the very bottom of an Office window. Often, the status bar displays useful information about the current file (Word, for instance, gives you a word count in the lower left-hand corner). But in most Office applications, the lower right-hand controls are the same: they give you different ways of viewing the current document, and they enable you to zoom in or out.

1 Pass your mouse arrow over one of the page view options in Word, Excel or PowerPoint to display the relevant ScreenTip.

2 Click one of the page view options to change the view.

? **DID YOU KNOW?**

The status bar can display the name of the current Office theme. The status bar also lets you see whether certain features are on or off, including signatures, permissions, Caps Lock, Num Lock, and many more.

3 Click the plus or minus signs to zoom in or out by one percentage point at a time.

4 Move the slider to the left or right to change the view.

5 Click and drag the resize handle to change the size of the window.

Add or remove status bar contents

- Right-click the status bar and choose an unticked item to add it to the status bar.

- Right-click the status bar and choose a ticked item to remove it from the status bar.

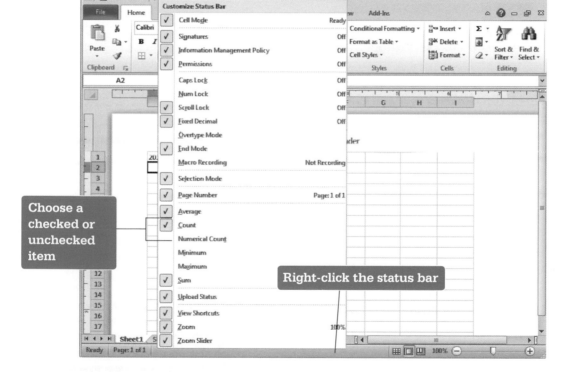

Choose a checked or unchecked item

Right-click the status bar

Change task panes

A task pane is a subdivision of the main Office program window. Task panes appear when they are needed or when you click the appropriate dialogue box launcher icon. The arrows next to Clipboard and Font in the ribbon each open task panes with controls related to them, for instance. Task panes can be resized and there is usually a Close button (an X) in the upper right-hand corner so you can close them when you're done. A related subdivision of the Office window, a window pane, is a part of a single window, such as a window that has been split into two sections.

1 Click the Clipboard arrow or another dialogue box launcher icon to open a task pane.

2 Click the down arrow and choose Move, Size or Close to move, resize or close the task pane.

3 Click the item displayed in the pane to select and work with it.

4 Click the Options button to view options for the task pane.

5 If necessary, use the scroll bars to locate Windows Photo Gallery.

6 Click Windows Photo Gallery to open the application.

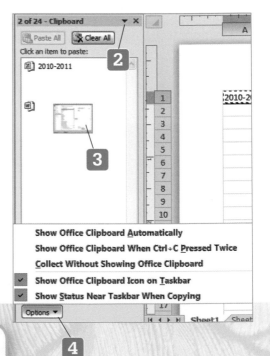

? DID YOU KNOW?

To open a window pane, do one of two things: either click and drag the Split button (which appears as a horizontal line at the top of the scroll bar), or click the View tab and click the Split button in the Window tool group.

Manage multiple windows

My daughters are always amazed at the number of applications and windows I have open at any one time. The fact is that I need to be doing several things at once, and chances are you do too. If you need to work with multiple document windows, you'll work faster and will be able to switch from one file to another more quickly if you arrange them efficiently. In other words, you don't need to fill your computer screen with a single window; you can display several windows at once and switch back and forth, making each one active when you need to work with them. Each window contains its own ribbon and work area.

Resize or move a window

1 Click the title bar of an inactive window to make it active.

2 Click one of the buttons in the upper right-hand corner to manipulate window size:

- Maximise button: click this button to make the window fill the screen.

- Restore Down button: if you have maximised a window and want to restore it to its previous smaller size, click this button.

- Close button: click here to close the window.

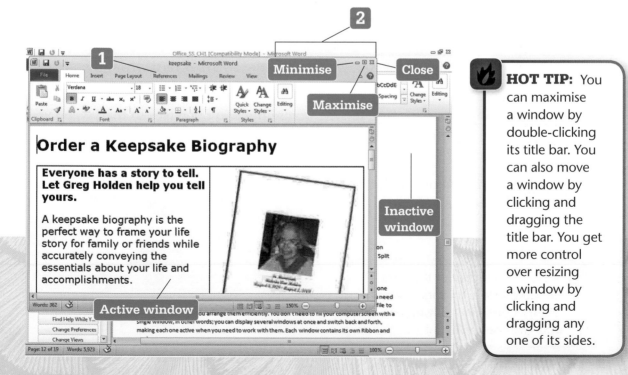

HOT TIP: You can maximise a window by double-clicking its title bar. You can also move a window by clicking and dragging the title bar. You get more control over resizing a window by clicking and dragging any one of its sides.

Arrange multiple windows

3 Open all the documents you want to work with.

4 Click the View tab on the active document.

5 In the Window tool group, do one of the following:

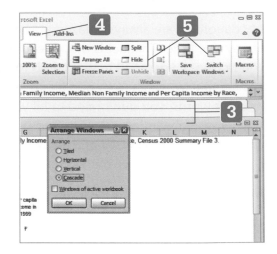

- Click Arrange all and choose an option (Tiled, Horizontal, Vertical or Cascade) and click OK.

- Click Switch Windows, and choose the document you want to work with.

- Click New Window to open a new window that contains the contents of the current document.

Arrange windows side by side

6 Open the two Word or Excel documents you want to compare.

7 Click the View tab in the Ribbon.

8 In the Window tool group, do one of the following:

- Click View Side By Side if you want to view the two files vertically at the same time.

- Click Synchronous Scrolling to synchronise the two open files so that, when you scroll one, the other scrolls along with it. (It's a great way to scan and compare the contents of two files.)

- Click Reset Window to reset the window position of the two files so they share an equal amount of the screen.

ALERT: In order for the Reset Window feature to work, you must first have the View Side By Side option chosen.

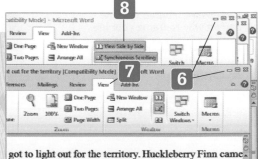

Create a document from a template

You don't need to create a new document from scratch. Office 2010 gives you a selection of professionally designed templates that you can use as a starting point. Templates work well when you know what your content will be but you don't have the time or experience to create a look and feel for presenting it in its best light. A template gives you colours, type styles and other attributes; you only need to add text and graphics. The New dialogue box lets you choose one of the templates that comes with Office, or allows you to pick one from the online library on the Microsoft Office Online website.

1 Click the File tab and choose New.

2 When the New Document window opens, do one of the following:

- Choose Recent from the column on the left to open recently used templates.
- Click Available Templates and choose a template that comes with Office.
- Click My Templates to choose any templates you have created and saved.
- Click Sample templates, and then choose a template from the samples section.
- Click an Office.com template category and then choose a template from the online list.

3 Click Create or Download.

4 If necessary, click the template of your choice and click OK.

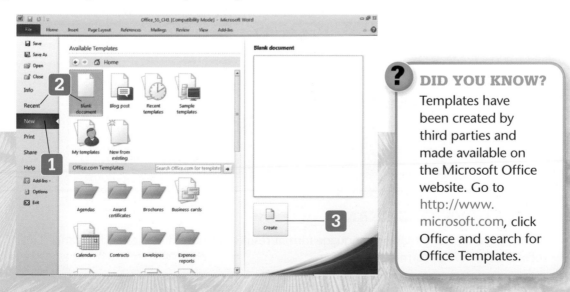

? DID YOU KNOW?

Templates have been created by third parties and made available on the Microsoft Office website. Go to http://www. microsoft.com, click Office and search for Office Templates.

Save a file

Saving a document, in any Office application, probably seems simple: click Office and choose Save, or press the Save button in the Home tab of the ribbon. But you have many other options at your disposal for saving files in different formats. You need to choose Save As, rather than Save, the first time you save a file or if you want to save the file with a different name. When you save a file, make sure you save it in the desired format. Office 2010 files are saved in a format based on XML (eXtensible Markup Language). You can also save in compatibility mode, which creates files in Office 97-2007 format (in other words, the document can be opened in Office 97 up to Office 2007.

Save a file in Office 2010 format

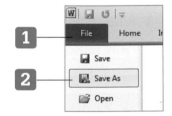

1   Click the File tab.

2   Choose Save As.

3   Click the Save in list arrow and identify the folder or drive where you want to save the file.

4   Type a file name for your document here.

5   Click the Save as type drop-down list and choose the file format for your file.

6   When you're finished, click Save.

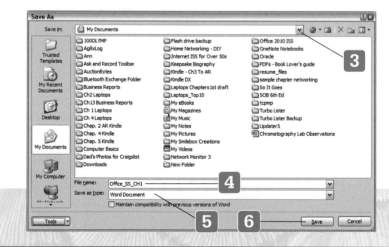

WHAT DOES THIS MEAN?

XML: The eXtensible Markup Language format results in smaller file sizes and enhanced file recovery than other formats.

Save in Office 97-2003 format

Compatibility mode is good if you are sharing the file with others who don't have Office 2010, but it disables new Office 2010 features that can't be handled by earlier versions.

7 If the open file is already in Office 97-2003 format, simply click the Save button on the quick access toolbar, press Ctrl+S, or click the Office button and choose Save.

8 If the open file is in Office 2010 or another format, click the Office button, choose Save As and choose <Program> 97-2003 Document.

Specify save defaults

9 Click the Office button, and click the <Program> Options button.

10 Click Save.

11 Choose the Save options: pick a default save format from the drop-down list, and a default file location.

12 Click OK.

Save an Office file in a different format

One of the biggest advantages of using Office 2010 is the ability to save a file created in one format in another. And because Office 2010 presents you with an integrated series of applications, that means you can save a file created in one application (such as Word) in another format (such as PowerPoint). It also means you can save a file as a webpage so you can view it online with a web browser. Excel also has a selection of specialised file formats, such as the binary file format BIFF12, which is optimal for large, complex workbooks.

1 Click the File tab.

2 Click Share.

3 Click Change File Type.

4 Click Save as Another File Type.

5 Click the Save as type drop-down list, and choose the file format you want. Some possible formats are listed in Table 1.1.

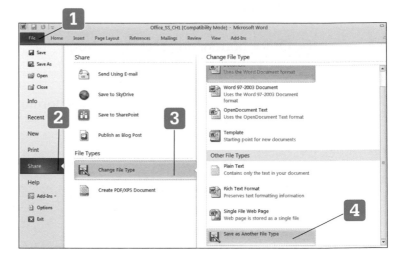

Table 1.1 Office 2010 Save as type formats

Save as type	File extension	Used with
Word document	.docx	Word 2010 or 2007 files
Excel workbook	.xlsx	Excel2010 or 2007 workbooks
PowerPoint presentation	.pptx	PowerPoint 2010 or 2007 presentations
Access 2007 database	.accdb	Access 2010 or 2007 databases
Excel 97-2003 workbook	.xls	Excel 97-2003 workbooks
PowerPoint 97-2003	.ppt	PowerPoint 97-2003 presentations
PowerPoint Show	.pps, .ppsx	PowerPoint 2010 or 2007 slide show
Access 2002-2003 database	.mdb	Access 2002-2004 database
Portable Document Format (PDF)	.pdf	Adobe PDF format
Web page	.htm, .html	Webpage folder containing an .htm file
Single-file webpage	.mht, .mhtml	A single webpage .htm file

Find help while you're working

Office 2010's Help utility is more than just a database of articles designed to help you use an application more effectively. It also connects you to Microsoft Office Online, where you can seamlessly search the Web for answers to your questions. You can search the Help utility by keyword or phrase, or browse by topic. When you search, you are presented with a list of possible answers, with the most likely one or the most frequently used one positioned at the top of the list.

1 Click the Help button, the blue question mark near the top of the ribbon.

2 Find the Help topic you need by:

- Clicking a Help category on the home page and then clicking a specific topic.

- Clicking the Table of Contents button, clicking a category and then clicking a topic.

3 Read the topic to find out more; click links to get more information.

4 Navigate the Help files by clicking the Back, Forward, Stop, Refresh and Home toolbar buttons much as you would do in a web browser.

5 Click Keep On Top to keep the Help window on top of other open windows. When Keep On Top is selected, the button changes to Not On Top to keep it behind other windows.

6 Click the Close button when you've finished.

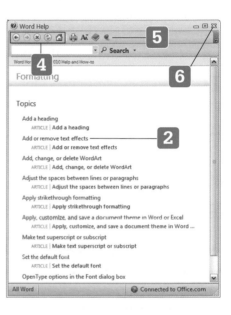

? DID YOU KNOW?

You can also press F1 to access Help at any time. To search the Help database, open the Help button by pressing F1 or clicking the Help icon. Then click the drop-down arrow next to the Search button on the Help window's toolbar. Then select the location where you want to search. Type one or more keywords in the text box next to the Search button, then click the Search button itself. You can then scan the list of topics to find the information you want.

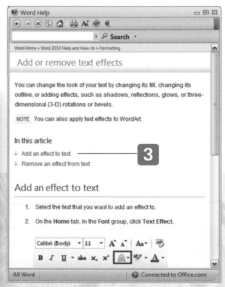

Change preferences

You are already familiar with the <Program> Options window from the preceding tasks in this chapter. It's the place where you can change how you want the application to save files, to display information and to handle specialised tasks. The Word Options window contains commands that control proofing, for instance, while the Excel Options window contains plenty of options for handling formulas. By setting preferences, you save time: you tell the program how to perform frequently used functions up front, so you don't have to do it repeatedly later on.

1 Click Start and click the <Program> Options button.

2 When the <Program> Options window opens, click one of the categories in the left-hand column to see what sorts of preferences you can set.

3 Click General to view frequently used controls, such as the option to display the Developer tab in the ribbon.

4 Click a specialised heading to view controls that are specific to the program.

5 When you've finished, click OK.

HOT TIP: You can also change language preferences for editing, display and help. If you have a language pack other than English installed on your computer. Click File, click Options and click Language. In the Set Office Language dialogue box, click the arrow next to Add Additional Editing Languages, choose the language you want and click Add.

Change views

If you use Word frequently for word processing, you're probably aware that the program gives you a variety of different ways to view information. These include Normal, Page Layout View and Print Layout View. Don't stick with the default view; at least take a moment to look over the options available to you, to see how you can view information. Even if you've used Office programs before, you won't be familiar with the new views.

1 Click the View tab.

2 Look over the buttons in the Document Views group and click each one in turn to view the available options:

- Word: Print Layout, Full Screen Reading, Web Layout, Outline and Draft.

- Excel: Normal, Page Layout, Full Screen, Custom and Page Break Preview.

- PowerPoint: Normal, Slide Sorter and Slide Show.

- Access: Form, Datasheet, Layout, Design and PivotTable.

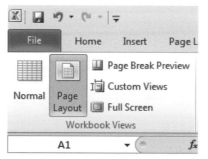

? DID YOU KNOW?

You can also use the view buttons on the View tab in the ribbon to switch between views. The View Selector buttons on the right-hand side of the status bar, near the zoom controls, also let you switch quickly between views.

! ALERT: If you use the View tab, you won't see view options for Access. You need to use the View Selector to switch between views for this application.

Update Office from the Web

Microsoft periodically releases software updates that improve the stability and security of particular applications, or of the suite as a whole. Each program in the suite gives you a way to manually connect to the Microsoft Update website so your system can be scanned for any needed updates. You'll then have the chance to choose which updates you actually want to install.

1 Click File.

2 Click Help.

3 Click Check for Updates.

4 Click Check for updates again.

ALERT: You need to be running Windows Explorer to view the Windows Update site. If you don't use Explorer, you need to turn on Automatic Updates on your computer.

Close a file and exit Office

Anyone who has lost information because they didn't save it or experienced slowdowns because too many files are open knows the importance of saving and closing files when they've finished working on them. When you've finished working, close the file; closing doesn't mean you quit the Office application altogether; you just free up memory so you can work on other files. Once you've completed your work, you can exit Office completely.

Close an Office file

1 Do one of the following:

- Click the File menu button and choose Close.

- Click the Close button, the X in the upper right-hand corner of the window.

2 Save the file when prompted.

Exit an Office application

3 Do one of the following:

- Click the File menu button and click Exit <Program>

- Click the Close box in the corner of all open windows.

4 Click the Save button on the quick access toolbar if prompted.

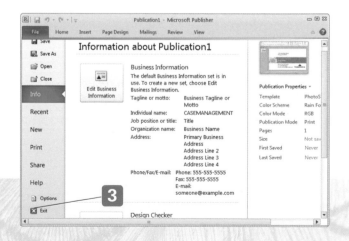

2 Working with text

Introduction

Text is an important part of every Office application, and is central to Word and an integral part of PowerPoint as well. The most fundamental aspects of working with text – typing, copying, cutting, pasting and spell checking – apply to all Office 2010 applications. Once you learn how to do the basics in one program, you can apply what you've learned to the others as well.

Office contains plenty of built-in functions that let you go well beyond the basics. The Find and Replace utility, which is found in nearly every Office application, is especially robust and easy to access in this version of Office. Spell checking can go well beyond notifying you if a word has a typo. You can use Office to suggest the right words and help you with your grammar as well.

Navigate a text file

One of the first things you'll notice when you open a file in Word 2010 is the presence of a separate column called a pane on the left-hand side of the window. This is the navigation pane; it's a new feature in Word 2010, one that lets you jump to a heading in a document and view the contents of a file quickly by giving you 'snapshots' of the headings or pages within it.

1 Open a file with separate headings. Headings are styles you assign to text: write a heading, select it and assign it one of the heading styles in the Styles section of the Home ribbon.

2 Click one of the headings to jump to it.

3 Right-click a heading to display a context menu with additional options. You can select the heading and all its contents or delete the heading and contents, for instance.

4 Position your mouse over the pane's border; click and hold down, and then drag the border to resize the pane as needed.

5 Click the bar to undock the pane and move it around on screen.

6 Click one of the three options for viewing the file:

- Browse the headings in the file.

- Browse thumbnail views of each page in the document.

- As this tab instructs, you can search for a term in the search box, or click the magnifying glass for other options, such as the Go To command, which lets you specify a page to go to.

7 Click the Close box to close the pane.

HOT TIP: You can show or hide the navigation pane on the View tab of the ribbon. Tick the box next to the navigation pane to display it; untick the box to hide it.

Select text

Even users who work with text on a regular basis (like yours truly) are unfamiliar with all of the tricks for selecting text. All of the Office applications give you shortcuts that make it easy to select words, sentences, paragraphs or lines. It's worth going through all of the selection options at least once so you can be aware that they exist; even if you use the same selection options (such as double-clicking or clicking and dragging) over and over, you'll surely find occasions where a special keyboard shortcut or other trick will save time and improve your productivity.

Use the mouse

1 Drag the mouse over a word or phrase and release the mouse to select it.

2 Move the pointer to the left of the line or paragraph until it points to the right, then click to select a line.

3 While the pointer is still pointing to the right, triple-click to select the entire document.

4 Press Ctrl, then click anywhere in the sentence to select it.

5 Triple-click anywhere in a paragraph to select it.

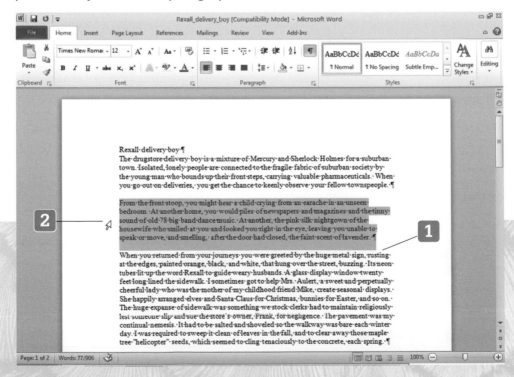

6 To select a vertical column of numbers or text, press Alt and drag the mouse arrow down and to the right over the text.

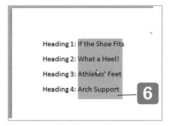

Use keyboard shortcuts

If you don't want to use a mouse (or don't have one available), you can select characters, words or longer text segments by using one of the keyboard shortcuts shown in Table 2.1.

Table 2.1 Text selection keyboard shortcuts

To select this	Use this keyboard combination
One character to the right	Press Shift+Right Arrow
One character to the left	Press Shift+Left Arrow
One line down from the current line	Press End, then press Shift+Down Arrow
One line up from the current line	Press Home, then press Shift+Up Arrow
An entire document, from the end to the start	Position the cursor at the end and press Ctrl+Shift+Home
An entire document, from the start to the end	Position the cursor at the beginning and press Ctrl+Shift+End
An entire document	Press Ctrl+A
A word, sentence, paragraph, or document	Press F8 once to enter selection mode. Then press F8 once to select a word, twice to select a sentence, three times to select a paragraph or four times to select the entire file. Press Esc to cancel selection mode

Edit text

Once you have learned to select the text you want as described in the preceding task, you can edit the text so it looks and reads the way you want. Most of the time, that means you'll want to cut, copy or paste text from one location to another. You can use keyboard commands for any of those functions; however, you can also use drag-and-drop to copy or move text from one file to another, or from one location to another in the same file.

Select and edit text

1 Use one of the techniques described in the preceding task, or drag the text cursor over your chosen text to select it. The text is highlighted in black to indicate that it has been selected.

2 Do one of the following:

- Type your new text to immediately replace the highlighted text.

- Press Backspace or Delete (Del) to delete the text and then type the new text.

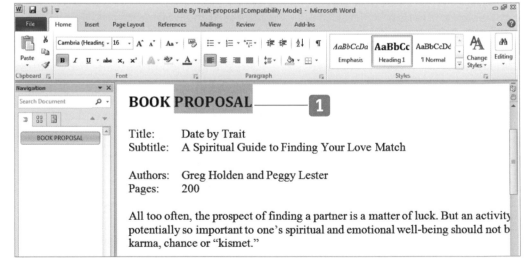

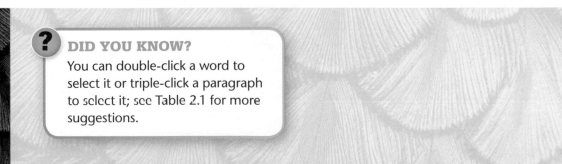

? DID YOU KNOW?

You can double-click a word to select it or triple-click a paragraph to select it; see Table 2.1 for more suggestions.

Drag and drop text

3 Make sure the text you want to move, and the destination point, are both visible on screen. This may mean opening two files, or displaying them side by side.

4 Select the text you want to copy or move.

5 Point your mouse arrow at the text, then click and hold down the mouse button.

6 Drag the selected text to the new location, then release the mouse button (and keyboard, if necessary).

7 Click elsewhere in the file to deselect the text.

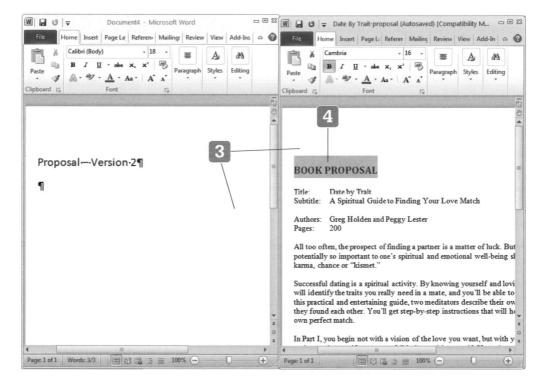

HOT TIP: If you want to copy text, while pointing at it, press and hold down Ctrl while clicking and holding down. A plus sign (+) appears to indicate that you are dragging a copy of the text not the original.

SEE ALSO: See the section Arrange windows side by side in Chapter 1 for instructions on how to show two documents next to one another.

Copy and move text

As you learned in the previous task, copying is different than moving. When you move text (or an image or other object), nothing remains in the original location. When you copy, you leave the original in its previous location. Another difference is that, when you copy, a duplicate of what you have copied is placed in the Clipboard. But the Clipboard can hold multiple items, not just one. You can use the Paste Special command and the new Paste menu to control exactly what you want to paste into its new location.

1 Select the text you want to copy.

2 Click the Copy or Cut button on the Home tab.

3 Click to position the cursor at the location where you want to paste the text.

4 Click Paste or press Ctrl+V.

5 To control the way you paste the text, click the Paste Options button and choose an option from the drop-down menu.

6 Alternatively, you can click the menu that appears when you paste the text and choose the paste options from there.

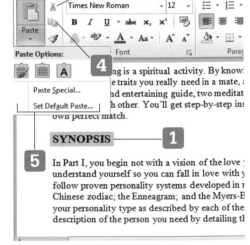

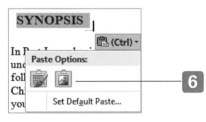

DID YOU KNOW?

When you paste text (or data) in Excel, a marquee appears around the pasted data until you press Esc. When you paste text (or data), it remains in the Clipboard so you can paste it again if you need to.

Use the Office Clipboard task pane

Usually, the Clipboard is something you don't see, but it acts as an invisible receptacle for text and other content you've placed there so you can paste it elsewhere. But you can see the items in the Clipboard and choose among them by clicking the Clipboard dialogue box launcher and opening the Clipboard as a task pane.

1️⃣ Click the Home tab if necessary.

2️⃣ Click the Clipboard dialogue box launcher.

3️⃣ Click the text you want to copy.

4️⃣ Click Copy. The content is added to the Clipboard task pane.

5️⃣ Position the cursor where you want to paste the text.

6️⃣ Click the drop-down arrow next to the Clipboard item and choose Paste.

7️⃣ Click the task pane's Close button to close it.

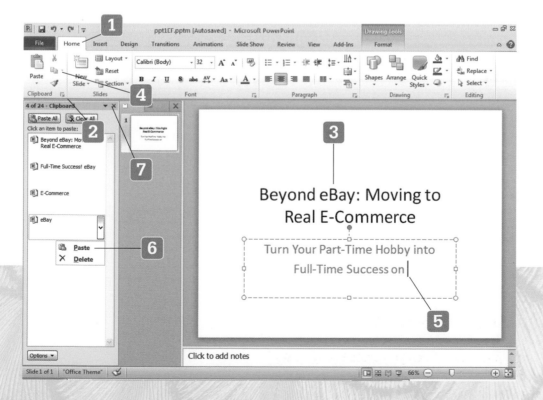

Use the Paste Special dialogue box

8 Click the down arrow beneath the Paste button.

9 Choose Paste Special.

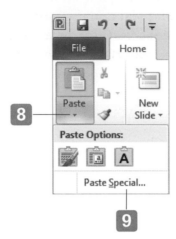

10 Choose the format in which you want the text or other content to be pasted.

11 Click OK.

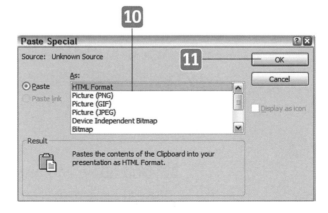

Find and replace text

The Find and Replace utility is present throughout the Office applications. In Office 2010, it's in a new place: the navigation pane. The basic purpose and the commands are the same. The Find dialogue box lets you find text, and the Replace dialogue box lets you replace it with different text. You also have the option of searching up, down or throughout a file, or to find whole words or text with certain formatting.

1 To find text, position the cursor at the start of the document, or at the point where you want the search to begin. Press Ctrl+F or click to position your cursor in the search box at the top of the navigation pane. Click the Find button, and choose Find from the drop-down list.

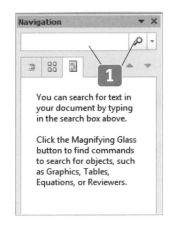

2 Type the text you want to find.

3 Click one of the instances of the search term displayed beneath the search box to jump to it in the document.

4 Click the up or down arrows to move to a previous or subsequent instance of the search term, respectively.

5 Click the down arrow for more options.

 HOT TIP: If the navigation pane is not open when you start your search, pressing Ctrl+F will cause it to open, with the search tab in the front.

Search and replace text in other Office applications

Although this chapter is about Word, it's worth mentioning the search and replace interface in other Office applications, which don't have a navigation pane. Excel, PowerPoint and other applications use the Find dialogue box with which you're probably familiar from previous versions of Office. This dialogue box also contains controls (a tab or a button, depending on the program) that let you replace words – you can replace 'dialog' with 'dialogue', for instance, either one term at a time or globally with a single click.

1 Position the cursor at the start of the document or at the point from which you want the search to begin. Click the Home tab, if necessary.

2 Press Ctrl+F or click the Find button on the Home ribbon (in Excel, the button is called Find & Select).

3 Type the text or formula you want to find in the Find what box.

4 Click Options to specify options to restrain the search.

5 Click Find Next repeatedly until you find the contents you want.

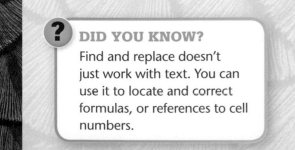

? DID YOU KNOW?

Find and replace doesn't just work with text. You can use it to locate and correct formulas, or references to cell numbers.

🔥 HOT TIP: If you are searching for one specific instance of a word or phrase, keep clicking Find Next until it appears. You don't have to replace text if you simply click Find Next.

6 Click Match case or Match entire cell contents to constrain your search further.

7 Click one of the options to find an item that has special formatting or that is located only in a row or a column.

8 Click Find All to find all instances of a formula or cell reference in a worksheet.

9 Results appear in the box below this button.

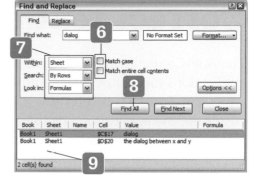

Replace text or formulas

10 Click at the beginning of the file or at the point in the file where you want to start replacing text.

11 Click the Home tab if necessary.

12 Click Replace or Find & Replace, depending on the program you are using. The Find and Replace dialogue box opens with the Replace tab in front.

13 Type the text you want to find in the box next to the Find what box.

14 Type the replacement text in the Replace with box.

15 Click Find Next to find the first instance of the specified text.

16 Click Replace to replace the first instance only, or Replace All to replace all instances at once.

17 Click Close when the message box appears when you have reached the end of the document.

Correct text automatically

The AutoCorrect feature you have probably noticed in Word is available for other Office applications too. AutoCorrect automatically repairs spelling or grammar errors as you type. AutoCorrect is helpful as it is, but the feature becomes more powerful when you customise the application's dictionary to include special terms such as proper names or brand names. You can also configure AutoCorrect to automatically add symbols such as the trademark symbol (™) when you type the letters TM, for instance.

Activate AutoCorrect

1 Click the File tab.

2 Click Options.

3 Click Proofing.

4 Click AutoCorrect Options.

5 Tick the box next to Show AutoCorrect Options buttons to display the blue button that lets you change AutoCorrect options.

6 Make sure Replace text as you type is ticked.

7 Select the capitalisation corrections you want AutoCorrect to make.

DID YOU KNOW?

When AutoCorrect fixes a word, a tiny blue box appears under the first letter. Pass your mouse arrow over the box and the AutoCorrect Options dialogue box appears so you can control whether or not you want the word corrected, or change other AutoCorrect settings.

8 If you want to specify exceptions that AutoCorrect should not change, click Exceptions.

9 Click OK.

Modify an AutoCorrect entry

10 Click the Office button and click <Program> Options.

11 Click Proofing and then click AutoCorrect.

12 Click the AutoCorrect tab if necessary.

13 If you want to add a misspelled word to the dictionary, type the misspelled word and the replacement and then click Add.

14 To edit the dictionary, select an item in it and click Delete or type the replacement.

15 Click OK.

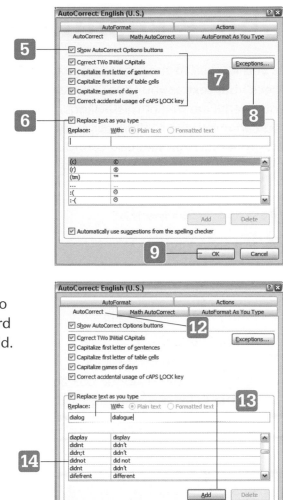

SEE ALSO: The Proofing tab in the Options dialogue box lets you use a custom dictionary. You might create a custom dictionary for a special purpose such as a scientific project. See Load a custom dictionary later in this chapter for instructions on how to create one.

Check spelling and grammar

As you learned in the preceding text, Office's AutoCorrect function has the ability to check your text as you type. You can also run manual spell checks to make sure your documents are free of misspellings. The spell checker is available in all Office programs. You can check the spelling as you're working on the file or when you've reached the end.

Check spelling manually

1 Click the Review tab.

2 Click Spelling. (In Word, click Spelling & Grammar.)

3 If a 'spelling check is complete' message appears, click OK.

4 If the Spelling or Spelling and Grammar dialogue box appears, do one or more of the following:

- Click Ignore Once to skip the word once.

- Click Ignore All or Ignore Rule to skip every instance of the term.

- Click Add to Dictionary to add the word to your Office dictionary so it won't show up as misspelled in future.

- Click one of the suggestions if you want to use it as a replacement, then click Change or Change All.

- Click AutoCorrect to add the corrected word (the word you have selected in the Suggestions list) to the AutoCorrect list.

? DID YOU KNOW?

Word's Spelling and Grammar function reports sentences or phrases that are problematic, along with words it thinks are misspelled. You don't have to do anything special to check grammar. Follow the steps for checking your spelling in order to make changes or ignore grammar suggestions.

5   Click Resume if you have stopped the spell check or Close when you are done.

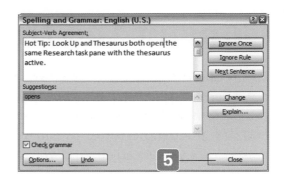

Change spelling and grammar options

6   Click the Office button and click <Program> Options.

7   Click Proofing.

8   Select or clear the spelling and grammar options by ticking or unticking them.

9   Choose Grammar & Style from the Writing Style drop-down list to check style as well as choice of words.

10   Click OK.

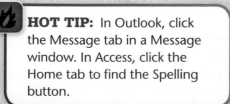

HOT TIP: In Outlook, click the Message tab in a Message window. In Access, click the Home tab to find the Spelling button.

Consult the thesaurus

The Review tab available in all Office applications not only lets you check your spelling, but it can suggest words for you as well. It's a function you might not even know Office can perform until you really need it: you're searching for the right word, and you can't find your printed thesaurus. Instead of scratching your head and guessing, use the built-in thesaurus you already have in your computer.

Use the context menu

1 Right-click the word for which you want to find a synonym.

2 Choose one of the following from the context menu:

- Synonyms: to choose one of a few synonyms Office suggests for you.

- Look Up: to look up the word in the thesaurus.

3 You can also choose Thesaurus from the submenu to look up other options.

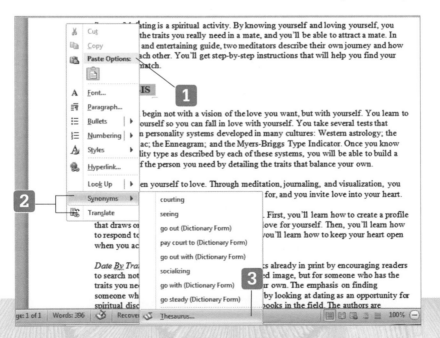

HOT TIP: Look Up and Thesaurus both open the same Research task pane with the thesaurus active. However, choosing Thesaurus is faster because it automatically looks up the term you have right-clicked.

Use the Research task pane

4 To highlight the text you want to look up, click the Review tab.

5 Click the Thesaurus button.

6 Click the list arrow and choose a thesaurus from the list if you want to use a special thesaurus.

7 Point to one of the words found in the thesaurus.

8 Click the list arrow that appears next to the word and choose one of the following:

  • Insert: to replace the highlighted word with the new one.

  • Copy: to copy the new word to the Clipboard so you can paste it.

  • Look Up: to look up the word.

9 When you've finished, click the Close box in the Research task pane.

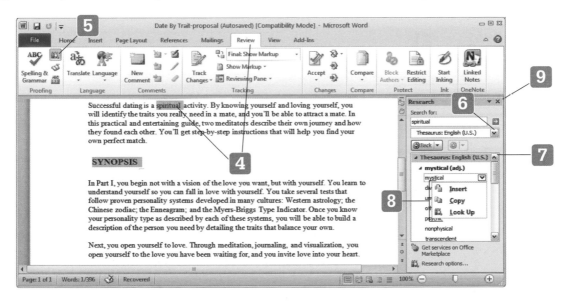

HOT TIP: In Outlook, click the Message tab in a Message window, and then click the Spelling button, to access the thesaurus.

DID YOU KNOW?
You can install thesauruses in other languages by looking under Research Options in the Research task pane.

Translate text

In the previous task, when you right-clicked a word, you might have noticed the word Translate as one of the options in the context menu. Office can translate text into one of a few languages for you. As you might expect, using a computer for translation is never as good as having a human being do the work, but at a pinch it can help if the word you're working on is simple.

1 Highlight the term.

2 Click the Review tab.

3 Click Translate and choose Translate Selected Text to open the Research task pane.

4 Choose a different language in the To box.

5 Enter a different word to translate in the Search for box.

6 Read suggestions for translation here.

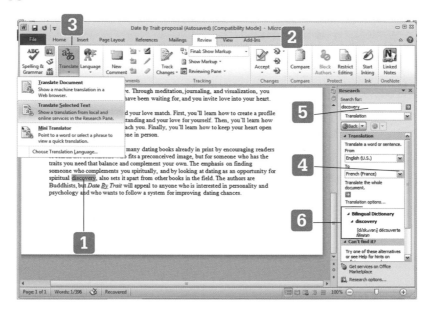

Import text files

If you want to go beyond simply cutting and pasting text and want to add an entire file to another Office document (for instance, a PowerPoint presentation), you can import the file.

1 Click the File tab.

2 Click Open.

3 Click the Files of type drop-down list arrow, and choose Text Files.

4 Click the text file you want to import.

5 Click Open.

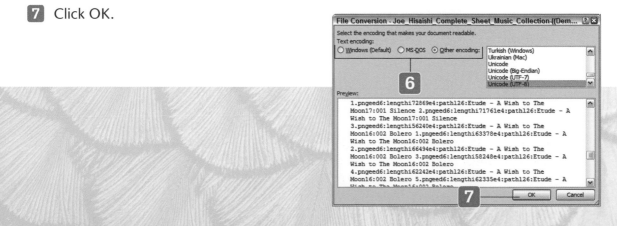

6 If a File Conversion dialogue box opens, click an encoding option.

7 Click OK.

Insert a symbol

If you ever want to add an em dash (—), a pound symbol (£) or a trademark symbol (™), you can do it quickly from any Office application. You can choose from a brief list of the most popular symbols in the Symbol drop-down list, or open the Symbol dialogue box to get a complete list of options.

1 Click to position the text cursor at the spot in the document where you want to insert the symbol.

2 Click the Insert tab.

3 Click the Symbol drop-down list.

4 Click the Symbol you want.

5 If you don't see the symbol you want, click the Symbol button to open the Symbol dialogue box. You can also click More Symbols to open the Symbol dialogue box.

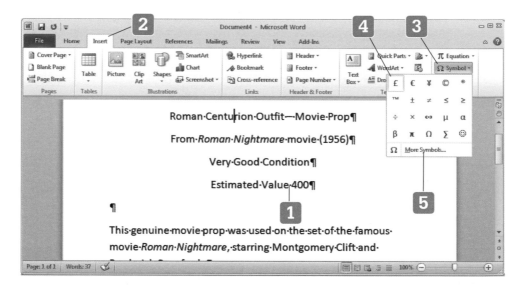

6 Click the Font drop-down list arrow to choose a new font if you want to view new symbols.

7 Click the symbol or character you want.

8 Click Insert.

9 Click the Special Characters tab to add em dashes and other common symbols.

? DID YOU KNOW?

If you don't see the symbol you want in the Symbol dialogue box, you can choose a different font from the Font list and try again. Different fonts contain different ranges of symbols.

HOT TIP: Scan the list of Recently used symbols at the bottom of the Symbol dialogue box to quickly add the one you want without having to look for it.

Create text boxes

Another way to insert text is to add it to a shape. If you use the drawing tools available in Office applications to draw simple shapes such as rectangles, circles or triangles, you can add text to those shapes. The text can serve as a label so the reader understands what is being shown. You do that by simply typing the text within the shape or by inserting a text box.

1 Click the shape to select it.

2 Click the Insert tab.

3 Click Text Box.

4 Click one of the text box styles. Click Draw Text Box if you want to control the size and position of the text box precisely.

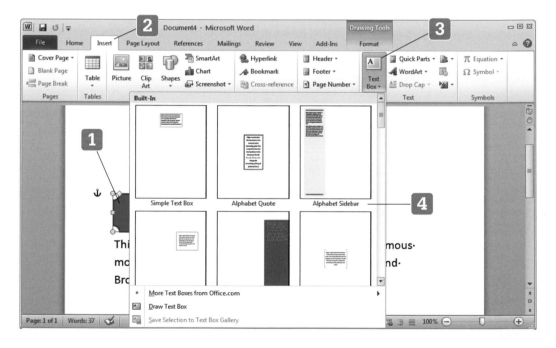

5 Click the dashed line around the text and drag it to reposition the text.

6 Click inside the text box to position the cursor so you can edit the text.

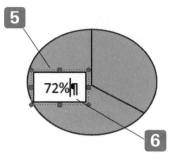

7 To format the text box (for instance, to change the border, or to add a fill colour), right-click inside it and choose Format Text Box.

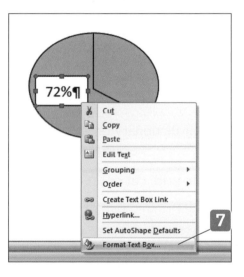

? DID YOU KNOW?

When you place text inside a shape, it becomes part of the shape. If you rotate or otherwise modify the shape, the text is modified as well.

Load a custom dictionary

A custom dictionary lets you look up the meanings of words in foreign languages. You can also create your own custom dictionary if you have a large number of special terms you use regularly. Before you can add a custom dictionary, you need to enable it using the Custom Dictionaries dialogue box. One particularly nice aspect of using Custom Dictionaries is the fact that any changes you make to them are shared with all of your other Microsoft Office programs.

1 Click the File tab and click Options.

2 Click Proofing.

3 Click Custom Dictionaries.

4 Tick the box next to CUSTOM.DIC (Default).

5 Click the Dictionary language drop-down list arrow, and choose a language for a new custom dictionary.

6 Choose options to create your dictionary or add an existing one:

- Edit Word List: click here to add, cut or edit terms.

- Change Default: click here to select a new default dictionary.

- New: click here to create a new dictionary.

- Add: click here to insert an existing dictionary.

- Remove: click here to remove a dictionary.

7 Click OK when you're done, and OK to close Word Options.

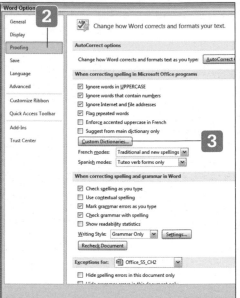

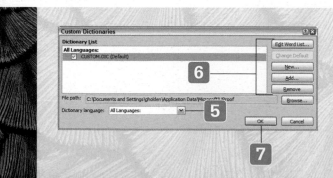

? DID YOU KNOW?

You can also add custom dictionaries to Access, Excel, PowerPoint and other Office applications by following the same steps.

3 Working with art and photos

Introduction

As they say, a picture is worth a thousand words – or cells in a spreadsheet, or pages in a presentation. Illustrations and photos make your content more compelling, no matter what program you're using. Microsoft Office doesn't include a graphics program as such, but each of its component applications gives you the ability to add and edit visual elements that make your information more compelling. Office 2010's drawing tools, in fact, are more powerful than in previous editions, so before you purchase an expensive drawing program, you might just try Office 2010 for your basic editing needs.

On top of that, Office also provides you with an extensive library of Clip Art – drawings and photos that have been created by professional artists and that you are free to add to your files. Office also gives you links to help you search through additional Clip Art collections on the Web.

Once you add a picture, you can resize, compress or crop it using simple drawing tools that are included on a drawing toolbar. This toolbar also enables you to create your own diagrams and illustrations from scratch. You also have the option of adding WordArt – text that comes in colourful and creative fonts that you can stretch into imaginative shapes and styles. All of these graphic tools are intended to make your documents more interesting with a minimum of effort. Explore them, and your work will be more interesting and more readable as well.

Browse Office Clip Art

Whenever you want to add an illustration to break up text or boost the attractiveness of a document, consider looking in Office's Clip Art files before you start taking photos or scanning images. Office comes with built-in Clip Art that you can add to your documents for free. What's more, you can browse the Office Clip Art files from within the application itself rather than having to open a separate graphics program. You can search the files by keyword to find what you need more easily.

1 Click the Insert tab.

2 Click Clip Art.

3 When the Clip Art task pane opens, type a keyword in the Search for box.

4 Click Go.

5 Click here and choose an option to narrow your search.

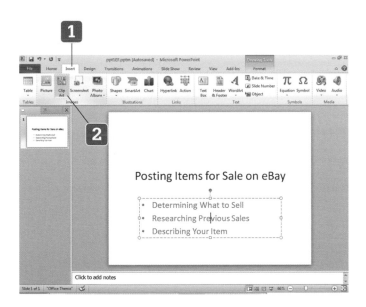

HOT TIP: If a Microsoft Clip Organizer dialogue box appears when you click Go, click Yes, to extend your search to the Clip Art Microsoft makes available to you online. If you're not online or want to keep your search options minimal, click No.

DID YOU KNOW?

If you click Organize Clips at the bottom of the Clip Art task pane, you open a browser that lets you view all the Clip Art collections by name and type.

Search for Clip Art online

If you don't find what you want in Office's built-in Clip Art collections, you can search additional Clip Art that Microsoft makes available to Office users on its website. You can also search for Clip Art available on other websites.

1 Click Insert.

2 Click Clip Art.

3 Either tick the box next to Include Office.com content before you do a search, or click the link Find more at Office.com.

HOT TIP: You can access the Microsoft online Clip Art webpage directly at http://officebeta. microsoft.com/en-us/images.

4 When the Microsoft Office Online Clip Art page appears, enter a term in the Clip Art search box.

5 Click Search.

6 Pass your mouse over the image you want to use.

7 Click the Download button on the context menu that appears.

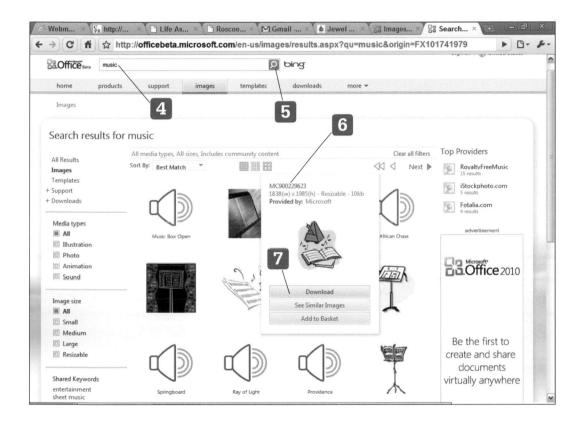

ALERT: Clip Art isn't always free. You can freely use the art that Microsoft makes available to Office users. But artists who make their work available online sometimes charge a fee or require you to give them credit. Make sure you read the 'fine print' before you use such images.

Insert Clip Art

Once you locate an image from the Office Clip Art collections in the Clip Art task pane, you have several options for handling it. When you pass your mouse pointer over the thumbnail version of the image, a down arrow appears. Click it, and you view a context menu that lets you perform various functions.

1 Click Insert.

2 Click Clip Art.

3 Enter a keyword in the Search for box and click Go.

4 Pass your mouse arrow over an image. Notice that an information box appears with details about the image file.

5 Click the down arrow.

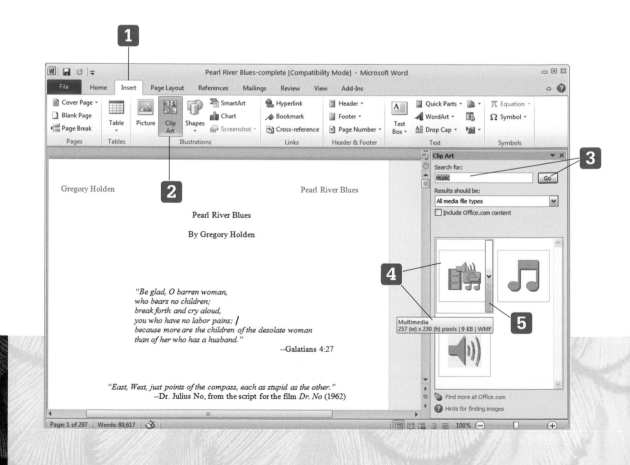

6 Choose an option from the drop-down menu list:

- Insert: to place the image in your document.

- Copy: to copy the image file to the Clipboard so you can paste it elsewhere.

- Delete from Clip Organizer: to remove the image from the Office Clip Art collection.

- Copy to Collection: to move the image from one collection to another.

- Edit Keywords: to add or delete keywords that describe the image.

- Find Similar Style: to find a similar image.

- Preview/Properties: to get a preview of the image and learn about its properties.

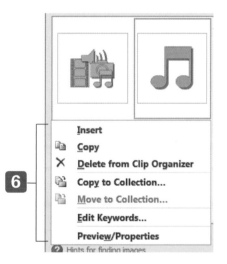

? DID YOU KNOW?

When you see details like 254 (w) × 232 (h) pixels, it means that the image is 254 pixels wide by 232 pixels in height.

HOT TIP: You can simply single-click the image itself to insert it in your document.

WHAT DOES THIS MEAN?

Pixel: a tiny rectangle that contains a bit of digital information. A digital image contains thousands or even millions of pixels.

WMF: Windows Media File.

Place a picture

Whether you have chosen an image from Office's Clip Art libraries or use a photo taken with your digital camera, you can easily add the image to a document. You can add a file from a CD-ROM, directly from your digital camera, from a 'flash' USB drive, or from a file on your hard disk. Before you add an image you can view a thumbnail to make sure it's the one you want.

1 Click the Insert tab.

2 Click Picture.

3 Click the Look in drop-down list arrow to locate photos on your file system.

4 Click an image file.

5 Click Insert.

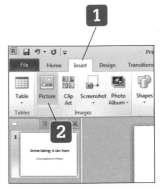

? DID YOU KNOW?

You can link to a file as well as insert it by clicking the drop-down list arrow next to Insert and choosing Link to File.

🔥 HOT TIP: Click the Photo Album button on the Insert tab to insert a series of images all at once.

Adjust picture size

When you first add an image to a document the chances are that it's too big for the available space. You have two options for resizing the image. You can click and drag the sizing handles on the frame that contains the image, for instance. But be careful to resize it proportionately or you'll distort its appearance.

1 Click the image to display the sizing handles on the sides and at the corners.

2 Drag one of the side handles if you want to make the image narrower or shorter.

3 Drag one of the corner handles to resize the object proportionately.

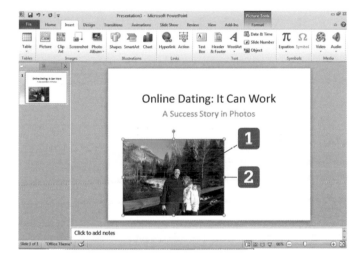

HOT TIP: Click the green circle at the top of the image and drag to rotate it.

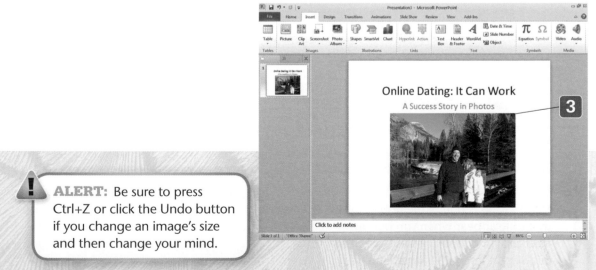

ALERT: Be sure to press Ctrl+Z or click the Undo button if you change an image's size and then change your mind.

Specify image size

Sometimes, you have a precise amount of space available to accommodate an image, and you need to be able to specify the size with precision. If you need to make an image an exact width or height, you can enter the size manually using the Format menu controls.

1 Click the image you want to change the size of.

2 Click the Format tab under Picture Tools.

3 Use the up or down arrows or type a size in the height or width dialogue boxes to specify the image size.

4 Click the Size dialogue box launcher to choose Lock aspect ratio or change other options.

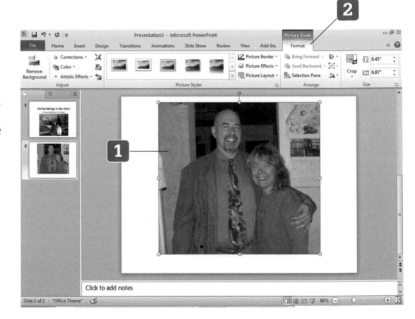

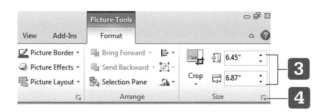

Add a border to a picture

If you are inserting a picture that needs to stand out from the surrounding text, a border can help. A border both separates text and images and calls attention to the image as well. The Picture Border button makes it easy, and also allows you to change the border thickness and colour to complement the rest of your document's design.

1 Click the image to display the selection handles around it.

2 Click Format under Picture Tools.

3 Click the Picture Border button.

4 Make a selection from the drop-down menu that appears:

- Choose a colour to apply it to the border.

- Choose No Outline to delete the border.

- Choose Weight and then choose an option from the submenu to assign a weight (or thickness) to the border.

- Choose Dashes and then click an option on the submenu to make the border dashed rather than solid.

HOT TIP: Choose More Lines from the Dashes submenu if you don't see the line style you want.

DID YOU KNOW?
If you don't see the colour you want under the drop-down menu or if you want to specify a colour by typing the R (red), G (green) and B (blue) values, choose More Outline Colors from the submenu.

Brighten up an image

Most photos that you take with a digital camera could benefit from some simple editing before you publish them online or in print. One of the simplest and most effective 'fixes' is to change the brightness or contrast of the image. By doing so you make the details of the image easier to view, especially if you plan to publish it on the Web.

1 Click the image to display the selection handles.

2 Click the Format tab under Picture Tools.

3 Click Corrections.

4 Choose one of the thumbnails of the image under Brightness and Contrast. The thumbnails give you an instant visual representation of how the image will look after changing brightness or contrast.

5 If you want more control over the brightness, choose Picture Corrections Options.

? **DID YOU KNOW?**

If you are unhappy with your changes, click Reset to return to its original appearance.

6 Click Picture Corrections.

7 Move the slider left or right to change the brightness one percentage point at a time. Do the same for contrast.

8 Click Close when you've finished.

WHAT DOES THIS MEAN?

Contrast: the difference between the dark and light areas in an image. Contrast is most often seen in photographic images. In black-and-white images, for instance, the light and dark areas are broken into shades of grey. By increasing contrast you highlight the difference between the light and dark shades and the image looks more vivid and dramatic. By lowering contrast you make the image softer.

? DID YOU KNOW?

The thumbnail images that show changes in brightness and contrast are a new feature in Office 2010.

Change an image's colour scheme

The Format ribbon that Office makes available has some surprisingly powerful features. One of those features is the ability to change the colour scheme of an image. You can change an image that is predominantly red to one that is blue, for instance, and adjust the brightness as you do so.

1️⃣ Click the image to select it.

2️⃣ Click Format.

3️⃣ Click Color.

4️⃣ Pass your mouse over each of the options under Recolor to see the color and brightness change interactively. Click an option to select it.

5️⃣ Click More Variations to choose a colour from a palette.

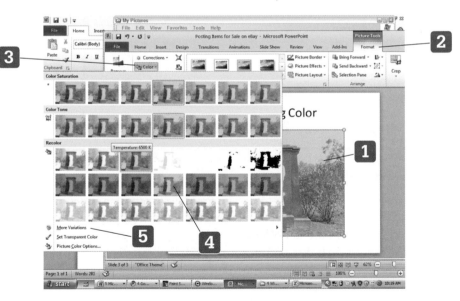

❓ DID YOU KNOW?

Some image formats (Graphics Interchange Format or GIF and Portable Network Graphics or PNG) have the ability to designate a colour as transparent. If you designate the colour that appears in the background of the image, the contents appear to be 'floating' atop a transparent background.

Crop and rotate a picture

Cropping is one of the most useful and effective options for editing a picture and preparing it for publication. Cropping not only focuses attention on the most important areas within an image, but it makes the image physically smaller so it fits better on a page. It also makes the file size smaller.

1 Click the image to select it.

2 Click Format.

3 Click Crop and then choose Crop from the drop-down menu.

4 Click and drag the side markers to make the image narrower or shorter.

5 Click and drag the corner markers to delete the contents you want to crop out.

6 Click anywhere outside the image when you are finished.

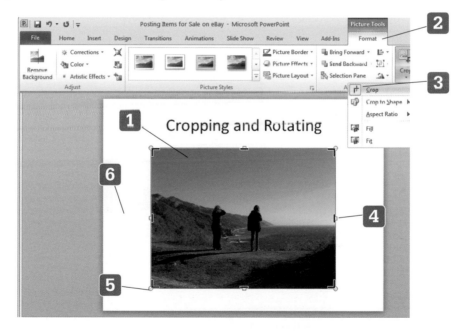

Rotate an image

Sometimes, the contents of a photographic image aren't precisely vertical or horizontal. Or, if you are inserting a piece of line art, you might want to rotate it so the contents 'point' one way rather than another. In either case, you can improve the image and the way it relates to the rest of the page by rotating it.

1 Select the image.

2 Hover the mouse pointer over the green rotate button at the top of the object, and drag it to rotate the object.

3 Click anywhere outside the object to save the rotation.

HOT TIP: You can rotate the image with precision (and make other changes as well) by right-clicking it and choosing Size and Position from the context menu. When the Size and Position dialogue box appears, click Size. Then change the degree of rotation in the Rotation field. Click Close when you are done.

HOT TIP: The Remove Background feature is new to Office 2010. It lets you remove the background of an image so it appears transparent. You can use this feature to edit images for presentation on the Web, for instance.

Create WordArt text

WordArt is an Office feature that lets you create text-based graphics. It turns your text into colourful art that you can slant, turn into 3-D or curve to follow a line. It's a great way to highlight an important message or make a page more interesting when you don't have photos or drawings to work with. In Office 2010, the WordArt options are more robust than ever before.

1 Click the Insert tab.

2 Click the WordArt button and choose a text style from the drop-down menu. A text box appears with placeholder text that you can replace by typing your own text.

3 Type the text you want to turn into WordArt.

4 If you wish, use the font commands on the Home tab to change the appearance of your text.

5 Position the text cursor in the WordArt text box if you want to edit the text.

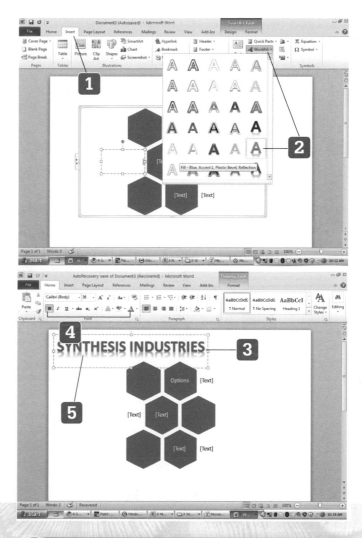

ALERT: Use WordArt sparingly. Too much large-scale, brightly coloured and textured text can distract from the rest of a publication.

DID YOU KNOW?

You can change any block of text in a text box to WordArt: select the text, click the Format tab under Drawing Tools, and choose one of the options in the WordArt Styles tool group.

Format WordArt

Once you have created WordArt, you should explore the many options for spicing up its appearance. These options allow you to choose new styles, change the way the characters are filled, and change the outline styles around the characters.

1 To change the current WordArt style, click the WordArt text to select it.

2 Click the Format tab under Drawing Tools or WordArt Tools.

3 Click the scroll arrows under Quick Styles to browse through additional WordArt styles.

4 Hover your mouse pointer over a style to view an interactive preview in your own text block. Click the style to select it.

5 To change the fill, click the Text Fill or Shape Fill button and choose a colour, gradient or texture option.

6 Click Text Outline or Shape Outline and choose a weight or dash style to change your WordArt outline style.

? DID YOU KNOW?

If you ever need to remove WordArt text, select it, click the Format tab, click the Quick Styles button and click Clear WordArt.

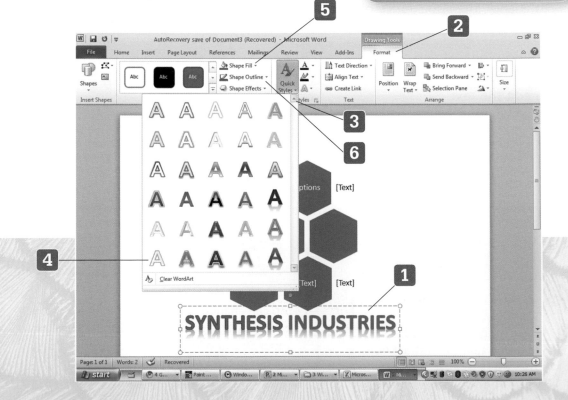

Apply special effects to WordArt

One of the best features of WordArt is the range of special effects you can apply with just a few mouse clicks and without having to do any fancy drawing. The available effects include shadows, reflections, glow, 3-D rotations and transformations.

1 Click the WordArt text that you want to edit.

2 Click the Format tab.

3 Click the Text Effects button.

4 Point to one of the Text Effects options, each of which has different submenu options:

- Shadow lets you choose a dark shadow area that gives the characters a 3-D effect.

- Reflection adds a faint reflected image under each character.

- Glow adds glow lines around the characters.

- Bevel makes the characters appear to be lifted off the screen.

- 3-D Rotation makes the images seem rotated and put in perspective.

- Transform lets you draw characters along a path or to make them appear warped.

? DID YOU KNOW?

You can always remove a style you have applied to WordArt by selecting the WordArt text, pointing to the style on the Text Effects gallery and selecting the No effect option.

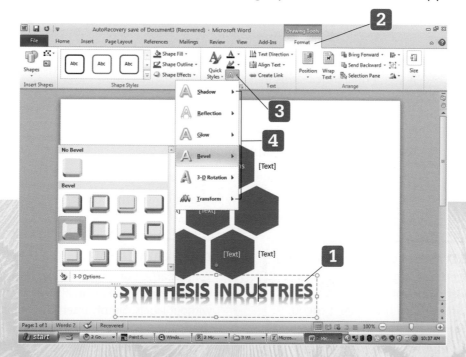

Create SmartArt graphics

SmartArt graphics are images that illustrate processes or relationships between elements within an Office document. A SmartArt graphic can illustrate a list, a series of steps in a process, a cycle, a hierarchy of items or a pyramid. If you ever want to graphically depict this sort of content, you only need to select a SmartArt object and then create the text to go along with it. SmartArt graphics types are listed in Table 3.1.

1 Click the Insert tab.

2 Click the SmartArt button.

3 Choose the general type of SmartArt graphic you want from the list on the left.

4 Click the specific style you want from the centre of the dialogue box.

5 Click OK to add the graphic to your document.

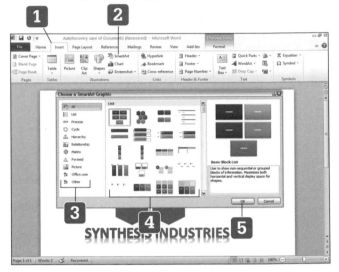

Table 3.1 SmartArt graphic types

Type	Choose this type to show...
List	Any set of non-sequential information
Process	A sequential set of steps in a process
Cycle	A process that proceeds continually
Hierarchy	A set of items in an organisation or a set of decisions
Relationship	Connections between people or data
Matrix	How individual items relate to a larger concept
Pyramid	Relationships that lead up to the top and down from there

HOT TIP: If you are working with PowerPoint, right-click the content placeholder and choose Convert to SmartArt from the context menu.

DID YOU KNOW?
Your SmartArt graphic does not have to contain text. It can be an abstract design without labels. Simply Insert the graphic and delete the placeholder text to leave it blank.

Draw and resize shapes

Office may not include a drawing application as such, but it still gives you the ability to create ready made shapes for you. You can resize, edit, add colour and fill the shapes freely to complement the rest of your document.

1 Click Insert.

2 Click the Shapes button.

3 Click the shape you want to draw.

4 Click at the place in the file where you want to add the shape, then drag to draw it.

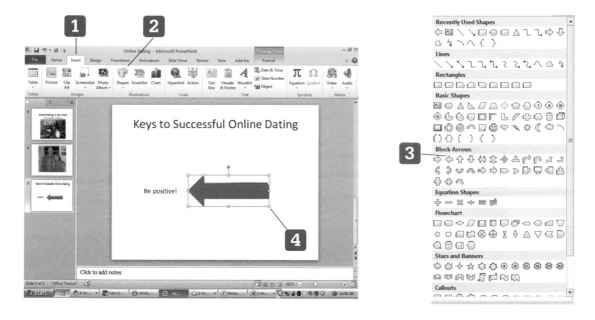

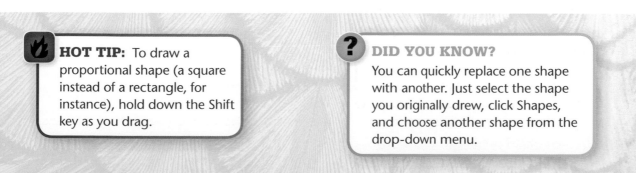

HOT TIP: To draw a proportional shape (a square instead of a rectangle, for instance), hold down the Shift key as you drag.

DID YOU KNOW?

You can quickly replace one shape with another. Just select the shape you originally drew, click Shapes, and choose another shape from the drop-down menu.

Align and distribute objects

Once you have drawn multiple shapes or inserted a set of graphics, you can arrange them using Office's alignment tools. You have the option of making two or more objects snap to a grid, or spacing two or more objects evenly. You can also align objects with a dividing line or other object.

1 Select the objects you want to arrange.

2 Click the Format tab under Drawing Tools.

3 Click the Align button.

4 Choose an alignment option from the drop-down menu.

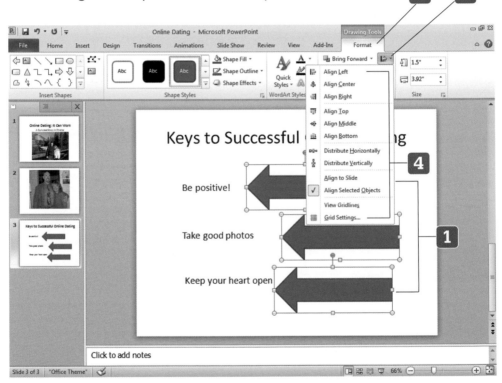

HOT TIP: Click an object to select it first; press Shift+click to select subsequent objects.

Manage your images

An Office tool called Picture Manager allows you to manage, edit and share your images. It gives you a single interface for locating your images. Once you open your files, you can use Picture Manager to crop, rotate or otherwise edit an image.

1 Start Picture Manager by clicking Start, pointing to All Programs, clicking Microsoft Office, clicking Microsoft Office Tools and clicking Microsoft Office Picture Manager.

2 When you first open Picture Manager, you are prompted to locate pictures on your computer. If your photos are not in the default location C:\My Pictures, you'll need to click Add Picture Shortcut.

3 Locate the folder that contains the photos you want to manage.

4 Click Add.

5 Click Locate pictures. Choose your disk drive from the drop-down list, and then click OK.

6 Click one of the View buttons to choose the way you want to view your images.

7 Click an image and then choose Edit Pictures if you want to change it.

8 When you're done, click the Close button.

6   **7**   **8**

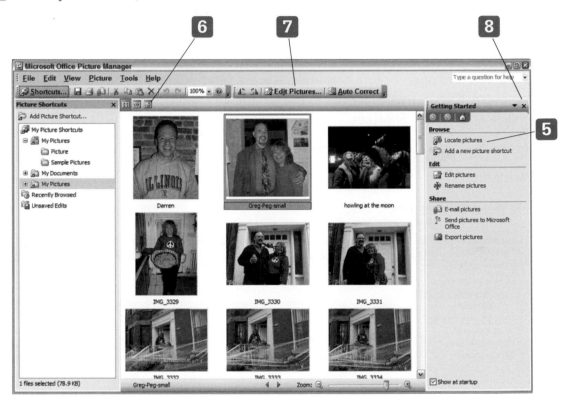

5

DID YOU KNOW?

The Edit Pictures task pane, which opens when you click the Edit Pictures button, lets you remove red eye from an image. You can also resize an image or even compress a picture so it takes up less disk space.

4 Applying themes and formatting

Introduction

Office 2010 gives you a variety of ways to format documents to make them look professional and businesslike. The first level of formatting is represented by the text commands that are common to all Office applications – bold, italic, underline and heading styles, and choices of typeface.

Once you get beyond the obvious formatting options, you discover that Office includes some very sophisticated tools for making documents look professionally designed. For instance, you can apply a design *theme* to your page. A theme is a coordinated set of colours and design elements that gives a document a look and feel. Office also gives you tools for formatting specialised content: tables, numbers in worksheets and comments you add to documents. All of these approaches are intended to make your words and data easier to interpret.

Apply a theme to an existing document

Office makes two kinds of design themes available to you: predesigned themes that come ready to use, and custom themes that you can create yourself. Each theme contains a palette of 12 complementary colours as well as preselected fonts and other special effects. You don't see the colours all at once; some are accent colours used for elements like drop shadows or hyperlinks. You can view and change any of the colours if you want to match certain colours you use in your other publications.

1 Open the file to which you want to apply a theme.

2 Click either the Page Layout or Design tab.

3 Click the Themes button to display the gallery of available themes.

4 Click your chosen theme to apply its fonts and colours to the current document.

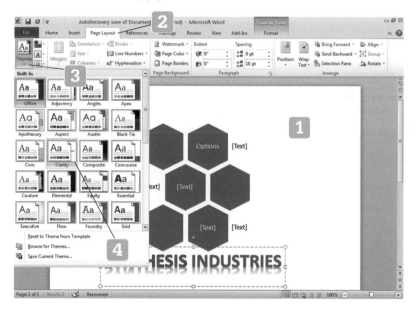

ALERT: If you are using Word, your document must be saved in Word 2010 format rather than as Word 97–2003 (Compatibility Mode) in order to use themes.

DID YOU KNOW?
When you pass your mouse arrow over a theme the colours appear in a live preview in the document that is currently open.

Apply a theme to a new document

You can also apply a theme as part of the process of creating a new Office document. When you do so, the background, text, graphics, charts and tables are automatically coordinated to the theme's look and feel. You only have to replace the placeholder text with your own content. You can always change the theme by choosing an option from the Themes submenu.

1 Click the File tab.

2 Click New.

3 Choose the template you want under Available Templates. Each template has a theme assigned to it: Equity, Urban, and so on.

4 Click Create.

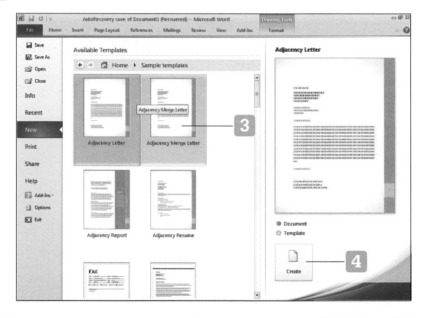

? DID YOU KNOW?

You aren't limited to the themes that come with Office 2010. You can also search for themes at Microsoft Office Online. Click one of the options under Office Online Templates. Follow the instructions on the website to download and apply Office themes.

🔥 HOT TIP: If you don't see the theme you want in the current set of templates, choose another template or click More Categories at the bottom of the left-hand column.

Apply a theme from another document

If you have created a custom theme or have a theme that you want to use in multiple files for consistency, you can quickly take the desired theme's attributes and apply them to a new document.

1 Open the document to which you want to apply the theme.

2 Click the Design or Page Layout tab.

3 Click Themes.

4 Click Browse for Themes.

5 Locate and select the Office document that contains the theme you want to use.

6 Click Apply.

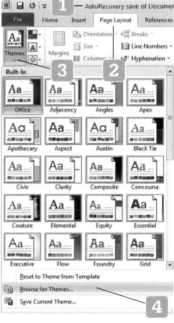

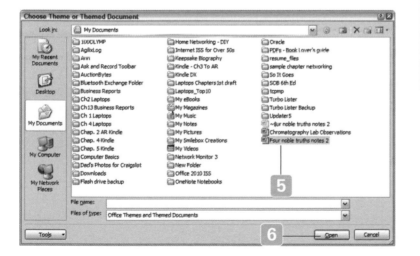

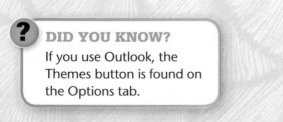

DID YOU KNOW?

If you use Outlook, the Themes button is found on the Options tab.

Change the default Office theme

Every Office document you create has a theme applied to it, whether you specifically select a theme or not. By default, the Office theme is applied to it, even if the file is completely blank. The Office theme has a white background, black text and other subtle colours such as blue for hyperlinks. If you get tired of the generic Office theme or want to consistently apply themes to all of your files, you can change it.

In Excel and Word, you need to create a new, default workbook or worksheet template.

In Word

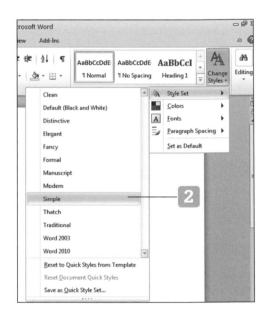

1 Press Ctrl+N to create a new blank document.

2 On the Home tab, click Change Styles, point to Style Set and choose the design you want to use.

3 Click Change Styles again, point to Colors and choose the colours you want.

4 Click Change Styles, point to Fonts and choose the fonts you want.

5 Click Change Styles and choose Set as Default.

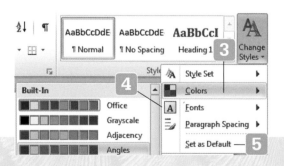

? DID YOU KNOW?

In PowerPoint, on the Design tab, right-click the theme you want and choose Set as Default Theme from the context menu.

In Excel

6 Press Ctrl+N to open a new blank workbook.

7 Click the Page Layout tab.

8 Click Themes.

9 Select the theme you want.

10 Click the File tab and click Save As.

11 Choose Excel Template from the Save as type drop-down list and click Save.

? DID YOU KNOW?

If you want to save a workbook with the default theme, name it sheet.xltx instead of book.xltx.

? DID YOU KNOW?

You can also create a default theme from an existing workbook that has the theme you want. Click the Office button, click New, click New from existing and locate the workbook you want to use. Click the workbook, click Create New, click Themes and choose the themes you want. Then follow the steps shown in this task.

Change theme colours

Each of Office's themes comes with a set of coordinated colours. However, you can incorporate your own colour scheme into a theme. It's a great option for anyone who is interested in graphic design, and who is familiar with RGB (red, green, blue) and other colour modes. Once you add colours to a theme, you can add it to Office's collection of colour themes so that it's available to any document.

1 Open the file to which you want to add new colours.

2 Click the Page Layout or Design tab.

3 Click Theme Colors.

4 If you want to apply a theme's colours to the current document, choose a set of colours from the drop-down list.

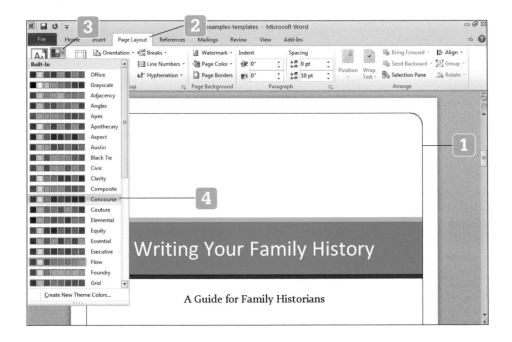

? DID YOU KNOW?

Each theme you customise is shared across all Office applications. For example, if you create a custom theme in Word, you also can open it in PowerPoint, Excel, Outlook or Access.

Create your own theme colours

If you don't see the colours you want in the drop-down menu that appears when you click Theme Colours, you can create your own.

1 Follow steps 1 to 4 in the previous section, then choose Create New Theme Colors.

2 Click the buttons for the colours you want to create – if you want to create your own text/ background colour, click that, for instance.

3 Either choose a Standard colour from the palette that appears, or choose More Colors.

4 Click a new colour from the Standard or Custom tab, and click OK.

5 Type a new name for your colour.

6 Click Save.

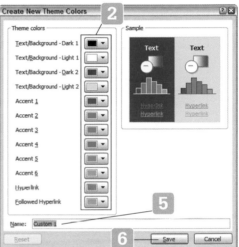

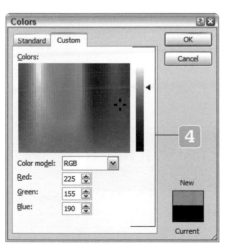

Change theme fonts

Each Office Theme has a set of type fonts chosen for it. You can change the fonts just as easily as you can change colours.

1 Open the document with the theme fonts you want to change.

2 Click the Page Layout or Design tab.

3 Click the Theme Fonts button.

4 Pass your mouse over the fonts shown to view a preview in the open document.

5 Click a font to add it to the theme.

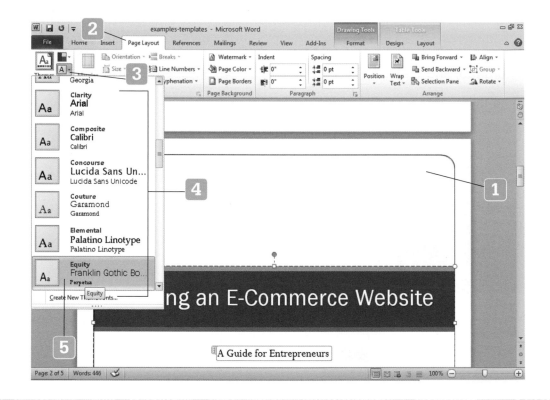

HOT TIP: You can assign colours, sizes and other attributes to theme fonts, just as you can any fonts you use in Office files.

Add special effects to themes

Themes not only include fonts and colours, but special effects as well. These effects include lines, charts, files and other elements that give flavour to your theme. Whether you're editing an existing theme or creating your own custom theme, be sure to pay attention to these additional features.

1 Open the document that has the effects you want to create or edit.

2 Click the Page Layout or Design tab.

3 Click the Theme Effects button.

4 Click the set of theme effects you want from the drop-down menu.

Create a custom theme

If you want to be able to exercise the ultimate level of control over your Office files, consider creating a theme. By creating a theme rather than designing the file from scratch, you gain the ability to quickly apply the theme elements from one file to another. This is ideal for an office, where coworkers need to create publications that have a consistent look and feel.

1 Press Ctrl+N to open a new blank file.

2 Click the Page Layout or Design tab.

3 Click the Theme Fonts, Theme Colors and Theme Effects buttons and choose the elements you want your theme to have.

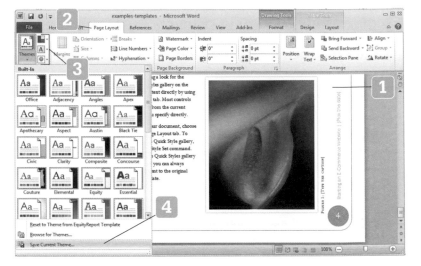

4 Click the Themes button and choose Save Current Theme.

5 Type a name for the theme you are creating.

6 Click Save.

Rotate and flip objects

The exercises to this point have examined design themes. You can also format specific design elements, such as images, that you insert in a file. One quick and dramatic way you can format an image or other object is to flip or rotate it. Office applications give you controls for performing these functions. If you flip an object, you turn it 180 degrees in the opposite direction. Rotating turns the object 90 degrees to the right or left. You also have the option to freely rotate an object.

1 Select the object you want to flip or rotate.

2 Click the Format tab.

3 Click Rotate.

4 Choose one of the rotation options to rotate the object 90 degrees.

5 Choose a flip option to flip the object.

6 Click and drag the green free rotation dot to rotate the object freely.

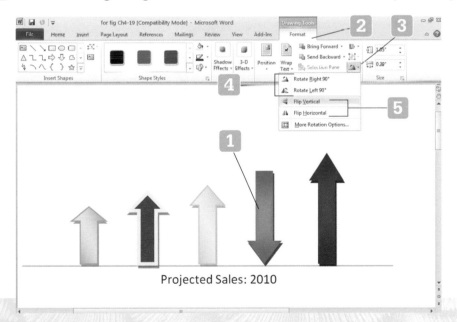

? DID YOU KNOW?

If you choose the More Rotation Options from the Rotate drop-down list, you can specify the number of degrees the object should move.

Make an object 3-D

Usually, artists need to employ some drawing ability to add the accents that give an object a three-dimensional appearance. But when you select an object, whether it is three-dimensional or not, you can turn to the 3-D controls on the Format tab and add such special effects.

1. Click the Insert tab and click Shapes.

2. Draw a simple two-dimensional shape, such as a rectangle, and leave the image selected.

3. Click Shape Effects.

4. Choose 3-D Rotation.

5. Pass your mouse pointer over an option to view the effect.

6. Click a 3-D option to select it.

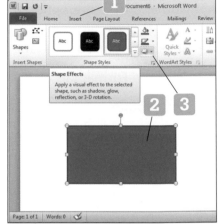

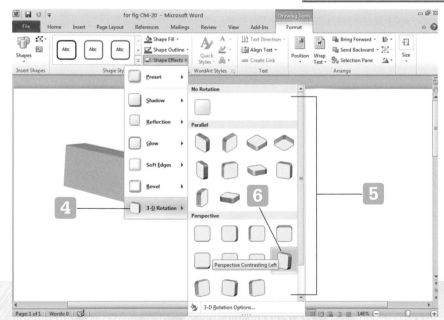

Change stacking order

Suppose you have multiple images in a file, and you want the images to overlap for a compact and sophisticated effect. You can change the 'stacking order' of those objects so that one appears atop the rest.

 Select the objects whose stacking order you want to change.

2 Click the Format tab.

3 Click the Bring Forward or Send Backward options and choose one of the drop-down list commands:

- Bring Forward brings the item up one position in the stack.

- Bring to Front brings the item to the top of the stack.

- Bring in Front of Text only works when the objects appear with text; choose it and the objects appear in front of the text.

- Send Backward sends the item one position down in the stack.

- Send to Back sends the item to the bottom of the stack.

- Send Behind Text only works when the objects appear with text; choose it and the objects appear behind the text.

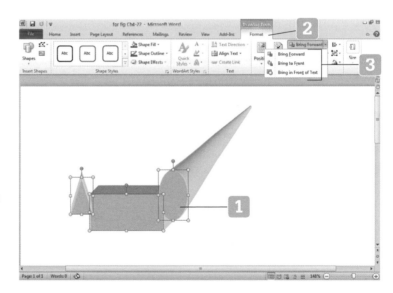

? DID YOU KNOW?

Bring in Front of Text or Send Behind Text only works if your document contains a mixture of text and graphics.

🔥 HOT TIP: Press Shift+click to select more than one object at a time.

Adjust shadows

Shadows don't make an object look three-dimensional, but they do add a sense of depth to the object. By throwing a shadow behind the object at a particular angle, the drawing looks far more professional than it would otherwise. Office's Format tab gives you a wide variety of shadow styles to choose from.

1 Select the object you want to format.

2 Click the Format tab.

3 Click Shape Effects.

4 Click Shadow.

5 Choose an option from the drop-down menu.

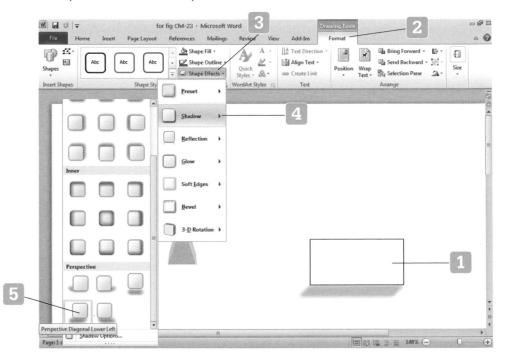

HOT TIP: Choose No Shadow Effect to remove the shadow effect if your object has one.

Format text in tables

Tables give you a user-friendly way to present information in rows and columns. When you select a table or individual parts (rows, columns or cells), the Table Tools heading appears above the ribbon. The Design and Layout tabs under Table Tools give you many commands for formatting tables the way you want.

1 Select the cells you want to format.

2 Click the Layout tab.

3 Click the Text Direction button to send text in the selected cells in a different direction.

4 Click one of the Alignment buttons to align text in the selected cells.

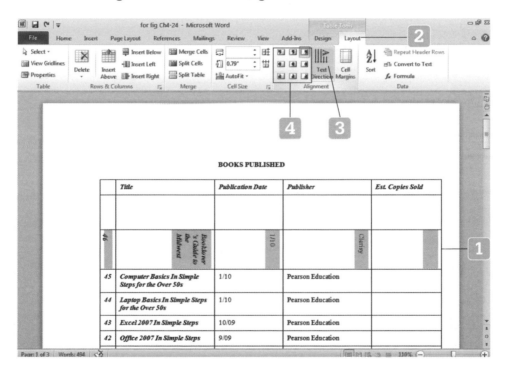

🔥 **HOT TIP:** Click the Select button on the left-hand side of the Layout tab to select parts of a table, or the entire table.

▶ **SEE ALSO:** In Chapter 5, you will learn how to create a table and begin working with data.

Use Quick Styles to format a table

Office provides you with a set of predesigned table layouts you can instantly apply. You find them under the Design tab; you can choose the one you want from a colourful gallery.

1 Click anywhere in the table you want to format.

2 Click the Design tab.

3 Click one of the scroll arrows to navigate the Quick Styles.

4 Click the style you want to apply to the table.

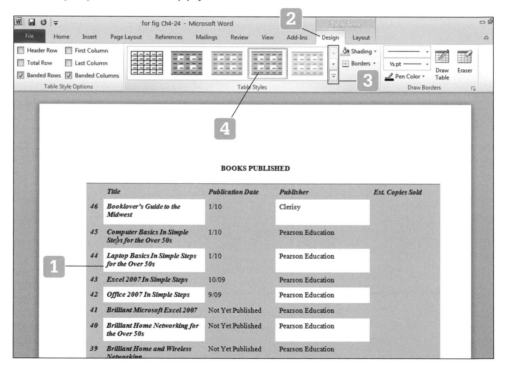

HOT TIP: When you reach the bottom of the table styles, click the More list arrow in the Table Styles group.

Format numbers in worksheets

Office 2010 provides Excel users with a new feature, the Number Format drop-down list, which lets you quickly format the appearance of numbers in cells. You are able to change the way the numbers look without changing the values themselves.

1 Select the cell or range of cells you want to format.

2 Click the Home tab if necessary.

3 Click the Number Format drop-down list and choose one of the available formats:

- General: no formatting
- Number: 1.50
- Currency: $1.50
- Accounting: $98.00 rather than $98
- Short Date: 10/17/2010

- Long Date: Wednesday, April 21, 2010
- Time: 1:20:00 PM
- Percentage: 33.33%
- Fraction: 1/2
- Scientific: 3.50E-02

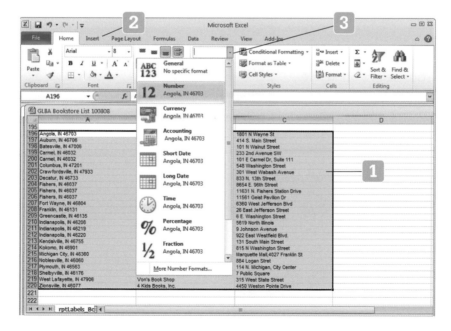

HOT TIP: Click the Number Format drop-down list, choose More number formats and choose English (U.K.) from the Locale drop-down list to change the default date format.

? DID YOU KNOW?

Just below the Number Format list, you see a set of numbers that let you do specialised formatting: Currency Style, Percent Style, Comma Style, Increase Decimal and Decrease Decimal.

Use the Format Cells dialogue box

You can also format numbers within cells the 'old fashioned' way. If you want a more familiar formatting interface than the new Number Format list provides, follow these steps to use the Format Cells dialogue box.

1 Select the cell or range of cells you want to format.

2 Click the Home tab if necessary.

3 Click the Number dialogue box launcher. The Format Cells dialogue box opens with the Number tab in front.

4 Select the options you want.

5 Preview your selection in the Sample box.

6 Click OK.

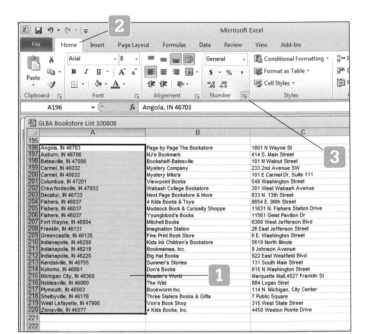

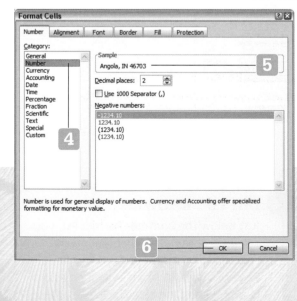

HOT TIP: You can create a custom number format if you don't see the one you want. Click Custom, type the number format code, and use one of the existing codes as a starting point.

Work with the Format Painter

The Format Painter is easy to overlook, but once you learn to use it, it can save you lots of time choosing formatting options from the ribbon. The format painter lets you copy all of the formatting attributes from one element to another. If you have formatted one paragraph in 14pt Helvetica bold italic type that uses small caps, when you type another paragraph and you have not done this formatting already, it can be time consuming to choose all of those options. The Format Painter lets you 'paint' them onto the new paragraph.

1 Select the cell, range or text that contains the formatting attributes you want to copy.

2 Click the Home tab if necessary.

3 Click the Format Painter button.

4 Select the text or click the object that you want to have the formatting. The formatting is applied.

5 If you double-clicked the Format Painter, apply the formatting to other objects as needed. Press Esc when you are done.

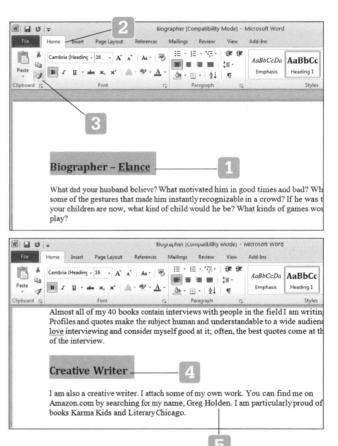

HOT TIP: If you plan to copy the formatting to more than one element, double-click the Format Painter.

DID YOU KNOW?

The cursor turns into a paintbrush icon when the Format Painter has been selected.

5 Creating a Word document

Introduction

Microsoft Office Word 2010 gives you all the tools and features you'll need to create business, personal and other documents that convey your message and make you look good as well. Word 2010 is more powerful than Word 2007 and far more sophisticated than previous versions. It contains auto recovery features that reduce your chances of losing information if your system crashes or you encounter another computer problem.

Word 2010 is also ideal for working in a collaborative environment. It gives you the ability to track changes to files and record those changes in comments that are easy for others to read. You can also compare separate versions of the same file to see what changes have been made.

Word is designed specially to work with text. But it has formatting features that go well beyond simple word processing documents. Word files are based on templates that contain predesigned fonts, colours and margins, among other features. You can modify the template styles to meet your publishing needs and create professional documents such as newsletters, invitations, posters and other eye-catching presentations.

Change document views

Word provides you with different ways of viewing a file so you can work with its content more easily. Each view corresponds to what you might need to do with the file: Print Layout shows you how each page lays out when printed; Full Screen Reading shows you the maximum amount of text all at once; Web Layout shows you how the file will look online; Outline shows you the contents arranged as an outline; and Draft shows you the file as a single long document without top or bottom margins (page breaks are indicated by a single dashed line).

1 Click the View tab.

2 Choose one of the five buttons in the Document Views group.

3 Alternatively, click one of the view buttons in the status bar. Pass your mouse pointer over each of the buttons to see what each one does.

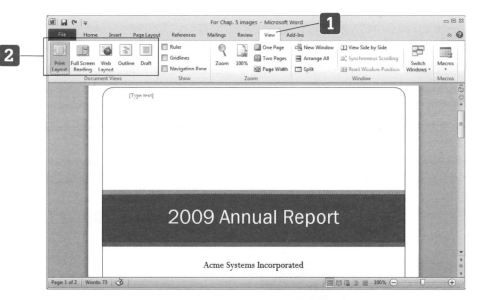

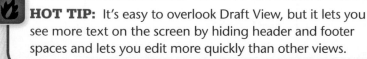

HOT TIP: It's easy to overlook Draft View, but it lets you see more text on the screen by hiding header and footer spaces and lets you edit more quickly than other views.

Make text easier to read

If you are having trouble reading text because the characters are too small, you can change to Full Screen Reading and then try some other view options to make the words bigger.

1 Click the View tab.

2 Click Full Screen Reading.

3 Click the View Options button.

4 Click Increase Text Size.

5 Click the Close button. You return to Print Layout.

> **HOT TIP:** Press the Esc key to move out of Full Screen Reading View and return to Print Layout.

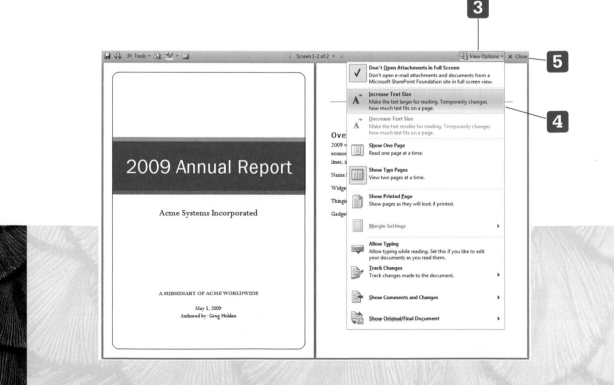

View multiple pages

Once you are in Full Screen Reading View, you gain access to the View Options menu, which gives you alternatives for viewing your content. One particularly useful command is the Show One Page or Show Two Pages options, which let you switch between these two views.

1 While in Full Screen Reading View, click View Options.

2 Choose Show One Page.

3 Choose Show Two Pages to switch back to two-page view.

4 When you've finished, click Close.

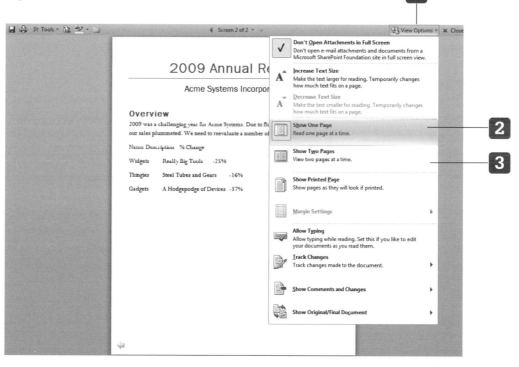

? DID YOU KNOW?

The View Options menu includes options to disable opening email attachments while you are in Full Screen Reading View. Other options include Show Printed Page, which lets you preview the page before it prints; Margin Settings, which lets you change margins; Allow Typing, which allows you to type in the document while in Full Screen Reading View; Track Changes, which lets you view revisions; Show Comments and Changes; and Show Original/Final Document, which lets you view either an original file (before changes) or the final version of the file (after changes).

Navigate a full screen document

When you are in Full Screen Reading View, you get a two-page look at a document. How do you move from one page to another, or view the headings in the document? You open the navigation pane, an Office 2010 feature that displays headings and subsections within a file. The navigation pane is available when you are in Full Screen Reading View. It opens on the left-hand side of the screen, whether you are viewing one or two pages at a time.

1 While you are in Full Screen Reading View, click the navigation button, which appears at the centre of the top of the page.

2 Click Navigation Pane.

3 Click a link to jump to the part of the file you want.

4 Click the right or left arrows to move forward or back one page at a time.

5 When you've finished, click Close.

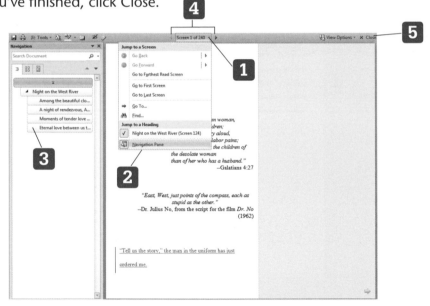

Set up the page

Every document has a page setup: a set of formatting instructions that describes how you view the contents and how they are printed as well. The page layout instructions that comprise page setup include its size (letter, legal, A4 or envelope) and its orientation (portrait or landscape). To set up a page's orientation, follow these steps:

1 Click the Page Layout tab.

2 Click Orientation.

3 Choose Landscape or Portrait to set the orientation.

4 Click Size to set the size.

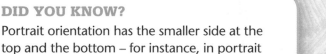

? DID YOU KNOW?

Portrait orientation has the smaller side at the top and the bottom – for instance, in portrait orientation the top is 21 centimetres while the sides are 27.9. In landscape orientation the measurements are reversed.

Set page margins visually

Margins are the blank areas around the four sides of a document. When you're working on screen, margins help make text more readable. But margins are more valuable when you print a file. The 'gutter' is the space between left and right pages – the right margin of the left-hand (or even-numbered page) and the left margin of the right-hand (or odd-numbered) page. Office lets you change page margins visually, using your mouse.

1 Click the Ruler check box on the View tab if the ruler is not already displayed.

2 Click the Page Layout tab.

3 Hover your mouse pointer over a margin boundary on either the horizontal or vertical ruler. Notice that markings appear to let you know the exact position of the margin boundary.

4 Press and hold Alt, and click a margin boundary to visually display the margin.

5 Drag each of the margins (left, right, top, bottom) to change them as needed.

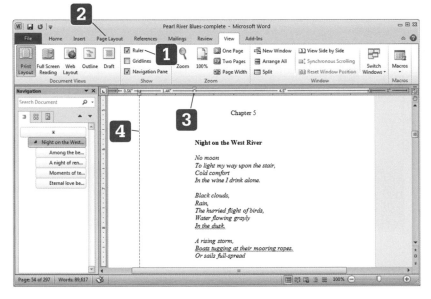

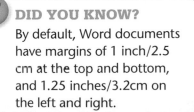

? DID YOU KNOW?

By default, Word documents have margins of 1 inch/2.5 cm at the top and bottom, and 1.25 inches/3.2cm on the left and right.

? DID YOU KNOW?

You can also use the Page Setup dialogue box to set up a page. Click the Page Layout tab, click Margins and click Custom Margins to open the Page Setup dialogue box.

Create an outline

An outline is a hierarchical way of organising a set of information into categories and subcategories. You can either create an outline from scratch while in Outline view, or you can convert the items in a bulleted or numbered list into an outline. These steps get you started on creating an outline from scratch.

1 Open a new file, and click the Page Layout tab.

2 Click the Outline View button.

3 Type a heading for your outline, and press Enter.

4 If you need to change the heading level to a higher or lower one, position the insertion point at the beginning of the heading and click the Promote or Demote buttons.

5 Move to the next line and type a subheading or item in the outline. Click the Promote or Demote buttons to change the level as needed.

6 When you've finished, click Close Outline View.

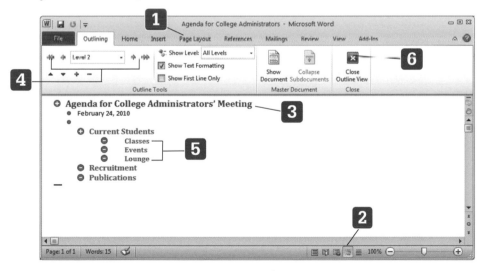

? DID YOU KNOW?

You can also position the cursor anywhere in a heading and click the Move Up or Move Down buttons (the green arrows at the top of the Outlining tab) until it is positioned correctly in the outline.

Add a new page or section

Adding a new page is an essential part of document creation. But not all page breaks are the same. When you add content and a new page is automatically added to accommodate it, that is a soft page break. When you manually insert a page break before the page is filled, you create a hard page break. You can also create a section break. A section is a separate document within a larger document; each section can have its own page numbering, margins, page orientation and so on.

1 Click to position the cursor at the point where you want to insert a hard page break.

2 Do one of the following:

- To insert a page break, click Insert and then click the Page Break button.

- To insert a blank page, click Insert and click the Blank Page button.

- To insert a section break, click the Page Layout button, click Page Break and click the page break or section break option you want.

3 If you need to delete a page break, click the page break to select it and press the Delete key.

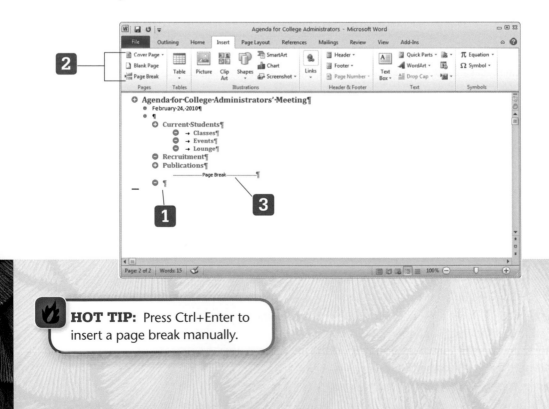

HOT TIP: Press Ctrl+Enter to insert a page break manually.

Add headers and footers

A *header* is content that appears in the top margin of a Word document page; a *footer* is content that appears in the bottom. The most common header or footer content is a page number. But headers and footers also typically contain a date, an author's name, the title of the work or the title of an individual section. Word 2010 offers a new feature – predefined headers and footers you can add with a single mouse click.

1. Click the Insert tab.

2. Click the Header or Footer button.

3. Choose one of the preformatted headers or footers.

4. Click Edit Footer if you need to modify one you have already edited.

5. Click the Design Tab under Header & Footer Tools to format the header or footer.

6. When you've finished, click Close Header and Footer.

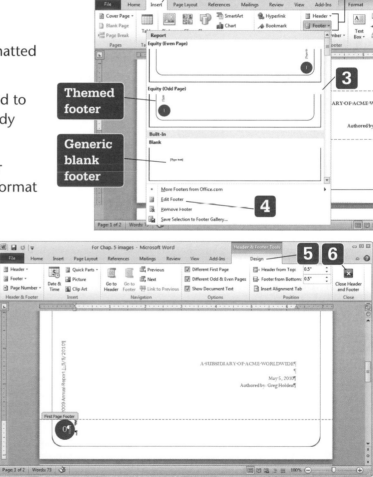

HOT TIP: Double-click a header or footer to edit it.

127

? DID YOU KNOW?

If your document uses one of the Office 2010 themes, the headers or footers you see when you click the Header or Footer button will have the same theme. A set of generic blank themes will also appear.

Insert page numbers

There's no need to add page numbers manually (typing them yourself on each page). Office 2010 lets you add page numbers quickly and updates them automatically as your content changes. You can insert preformatted page numbers, and ensure that your document uses different page number positioning on odd and even pages.

1 Click the Insert tab.

2 Click Page Number.

3 Click one of the positioning options and specific submenu designs.

4 Click the Design tab under Header and Footer Tools to format the page number.

5 Tick these boxes to change formatting depending on the page number.

6 When you've finished, click Close Header and Footer.

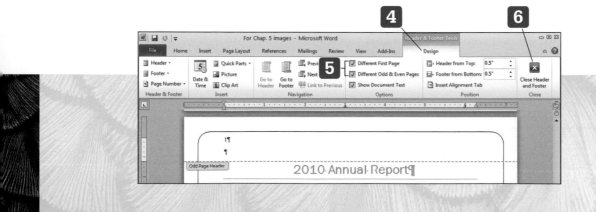

Add the date and time

Office 2010 keeps track of the current date and time as recorded by your computer's internal calendar and clock. You not only are able to insert the current date and time, but insert it in any installed language. Adding a 'timestamp' makes it easier to track different versions of your file.

1 Click the Insert tab.

2 Click to position the cursor where you want the date and time to appear.

3 Click the Design tab under Header & Footer Tools.

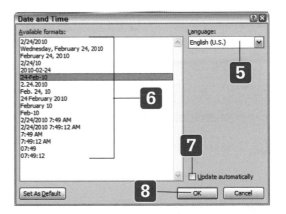

4 Click the Date & Time button.

5 Click the Language and select the language if needed.

6 Choose the desired format.

7 Check the Update automatically box to automatically update the date or time.

8 Click OK and click the Close Header and Footer button when you've finished.

ALERT: Be sure to first display or insert a header or footer and position the cursor there before inserting the date and time.

Find and replace formatting

Word 2010's Find and Replace tool is powerful, allowing you to find text and other characters, and to limit your search to whole words. It also gives you a way to find elements that have particular formatting attributes.

1 Click the Home tab if necessary.

2 Click Find and select one of the options from the drop-down menu: Find if you simply want to locate content, or Replace if you need to replace something.

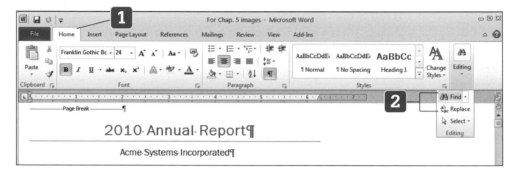

3 Click No Formatting to clear any previous formatting choices.

4 Click More, click Format and choose the formatting you want to find.

5 Click Find Next to find the next instance of formatted text.

6 Click OK and then click Close.

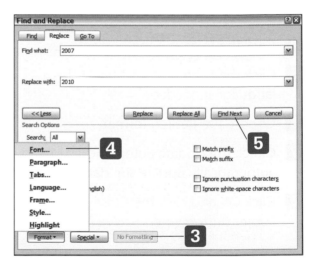

? DID YOU KNOW?

When you search for formatting, you don't necessarily have to search for specific text. You can also search for bookmarks, comments or other secondary elements in a Word file. Click the Home tab, click the down arrow next to Find, click Go To, select the type of item you want to find and click Next.

SEE ALSO: See Chapter 2 for the basics on finding and replacing text using the new navigation pane in Office 2010.

Set paragraph tabs

Tab stops in a Word file control how text or data aligns relative to the document margins. A tab stop defines where the content should align when you press the tab key. By default, tab stops are set at every half inch (1.3 cm). You can set one of four tab stops: left, right, centre and decimal. The Tab button to the left of the horizontal ruler lets you switch between the different types of tabs.

1 Select one or more paragraphs that you want to align with the tab stop.

2 Click the Tab button repeatedly until you see the type of tab stop you want.

3 Click the ruler at the point where you want to insert the table stop.

4 Drag the tab stop to the right or left to adjust its position.

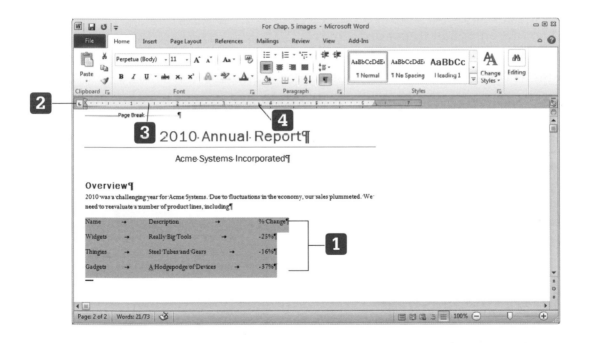

Change character spacing

You can go weeks or months without thinking about adjusting the default character spacing – the spacing between individual characters in text. You have two options: adjust the spacing between all characters in a uniform way using the Font dialogue box commands, or by changing the kerning for individual characters. Kerning is the print and design term for character spacing.

1 Select the text you want to format.

2 Click the Home tab if needed.

3 Click the Font dialogue box launcher.

4 Click the Advanced tab.

5 Click the Spacing drop-down list and choose an option (Expanded, for instance). Click the up or down arrows to choose the amount of change.

6 View the results in the preview area.

7 Click OK.

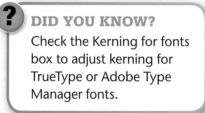

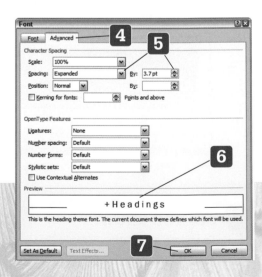

? DID YOU KNOW?
Check the Kerning for fonts box to adjust kerning for TrueType or Adobe Type Manager fonts.

! ALERT: Kerning only works with TrueType or Adobe Type Manager fonts.

Apply a Style Set

One of Word 2010's new features is the ability to add predefined style sets that help you format an entire document. Each Style Set has its own colours, fonts and other formatting combinations. The Style Sets have names that describe how they look: Classic, Elegant, Simple, Modern, Formal, Fancy and Distinctive.

1 Click the Home tab if necessary.

2 Click Change Styles.

3 Point to Style Set, and choose the style you want.

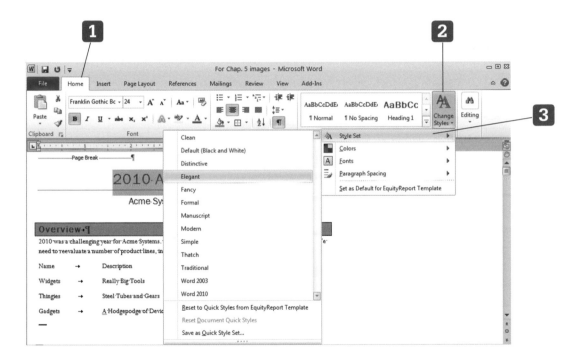

DID YOU KNOW?

The Reset Document Quick Steps option beneath the list of Style Sets lets you reset the document back to use Quick Styles – the styles that are shown in the gallery in the Home ribbon.

Create or modify a style

Word 2010 comes with an extensive set of built-in styles, but if you need to create a style that's not included, you can do so easily. When you create a new style and save it with your own name, you can quickly apply it to paragraphs or characters in other files. And whether you are working with a style of your own creation or a Quick Style that Word 2010 has provided, you can easily modify that style to your needs.

1 Create text that has the formatting you want to save as a style, and select that text.

2 On the Home tab, click the More arrow in the Styles group and choose Save Selection as a New Quick Style.

3 Type a short and easy-to-remember name for your style.

4 Click Modify.

5 Click Style type and choose either Paragraph or Character to denote the type of formatting you want the style to have.

6 Select any formatting options you want.

7 Tick the Add to Quick Style list box and click OK twice.

Modify a style

8 On the Home tab, click the More list arrow in the Styles group.

9 Right-click the name of the style you want to modify, and choose Modify.

10 Change the formatting attributes you want to modify.

11 Click Format and choose the type of formatting you want to modify (font or paragraph).

12 When you've finished, click OK.

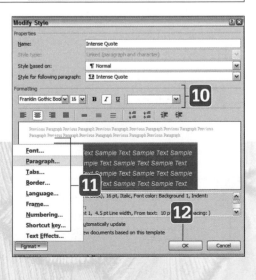

Create bulleted and numbered lists

Lists give you a useful way to break up long blocks of text and call attention to especially important items or to step-by-step instructions. Word makes it easy for you to go beyond a simple single-level list and include lists with many different levels.

1 Click to position the cursor at the spot where you want to create a list.

2 Click the Home tab if necessary.

3 Click the down arrow next to the Bullets or Numbering button, and choose a style from the drop-down menu.

4 Type the first item in the list, and press Enter. Continue typing list items until you are done.

5 Click the Bullets or Numbering button again to end the list.

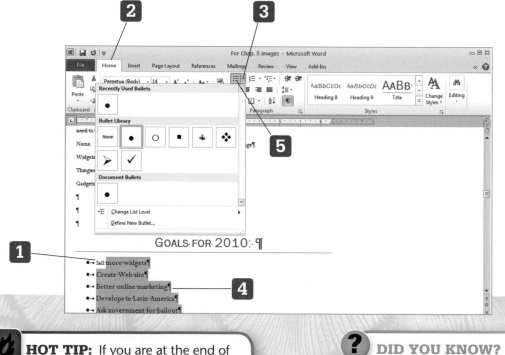

HOT TIP: If you are at the end of a list and mistakenly type a bullet or number, press Backspace repeatedly until you are at the left margin and can begin typing regular text.

DID YOU KNOW?

To create a sublevel under the main list level, position the cursor before an item and press the Tab key.

Modify bullet or number styles

By default, bullets in Word appear as black dots, and numbers appear as Roman numerals 1, 2, 3 and so on. You have many other options to choose from; you can also have a list start at a number other than 1 or change the alignment of list items.

1. Select the entire list you created.

2. Click the Home tab.

3. Click the down arrow next to Bullets or Numbering.

4. Choose Define New Bullet or Define New Number Format.

5. Change the alignment or choose a graphic object.

6. Click OK.

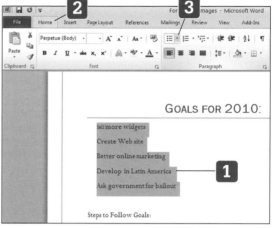

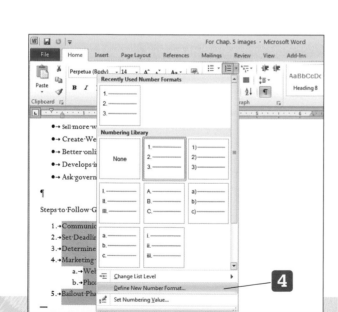

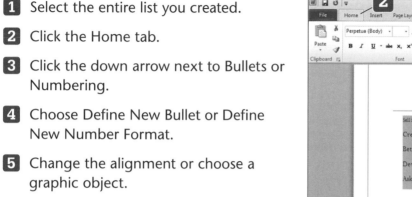

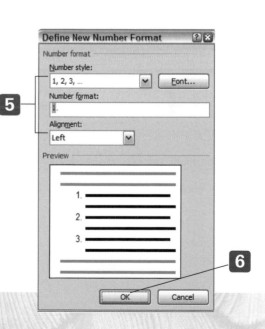

HOT TIP: If you have checked the automatic bulleted or numbered list items in Word Options you only have to format the first item in the list. When you type subsequent items, they will be automatically formatted for you.

Create a table

In the previous chapter, you learned how to format tables. Tables are arrangements of data or text in a grid consisting of rows, columns and cells. But how do you create a table in the first place? The easiest way is to draw the table's layouts. You can also convert text into a table, provided you have separated the text by tabs.

1 Select the text that you want to convert into a table.

2 Click the Insert tab.

3 Click Table, and choose Convert Text to Table.

4 Alternatively, if you want to draw the table, click and drag over the table cells shown. The cells you have selected turn dark; if you have three rows of three dark cells each, you'll have a table with three rows and three columns.

5 Enter the number of rows and columns, and choose other formatting as needed.

6 Click OK when you're done.

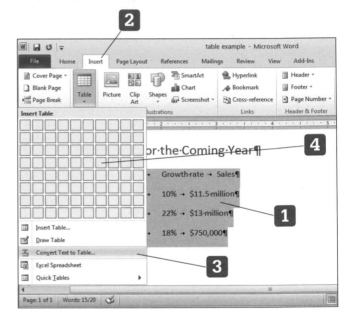

SEE ALSO: See Chapter 4 for some quick formatting options for tables.

6 Working with Excel speadsheets

Introduction

Excel 2010 makes it easier than ever to create workbooks and format the worksheets within them. On a worksheet, you can add or remove rows, cells and columns as needed. You can resize and move these elements using ribbon commands. And you can add worksheets or move them by clicking and dragging tabs at the bottom of the Excel window.

Excel, like other Office 2010 applications, is ideally suited for situations when you need to create a framework for data, and when you want to preserve the framework for consistency while changing the data. The pre-prepared templates that come with Excel will be perfect for your business or personal needs.

Some Excel features help you do your work more efficiently by avoiding trouble. Formula AutoCorrect is an example: when you press the equals sign (=), Formula AutoCorrect is automatically activated. As you type your formula, valid (and correctly spelled) commands appear in a convenient drop-down list. This chapter describes basic operations you can perform with Excel simply and easily.

Select cells

Before you can enter data in a cell, move it or apply a formula to it, you need to select it. Selecting a single cell is easy; you just click it. To select a range, you use Shift+click. But you can also drag to select cells and use some nifty keyboard shortcuts as well.

1 Select the first cell in the range by clicking it.

2 Hold down the Shift key and click the last cell in the range to select all the cells between them. (You can also drag to select a range of contiguous cells.)

3 Click the first cell or range of cells you want to select.

4 Press and hold down the Ctrl key and select other cells in the worksheet that are not contiguous.

? DID YOU KNOW?

When you select a range of contiguous cells, the top-left cell is surrounded by the cell pointer; the rest of the cells are highlighted.

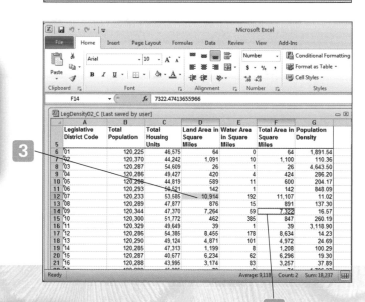

! ALERT: The Shift+click method only works if the cells are contiguous. If the cells you want to click are non-contiguous, press and hold down the Ctrl key while selecting the cells.

Jump to a specific location

The easy way to navigate through the cells in a worksheet is to point your mouse and click. For most situations, this is all you'll need. If you have an IntelliMouse, you can move the wheel with your finger to move through cells; the usual pointer changes shape and lets you move through the worksheet as you drag your mouse. Once in a while, though, the Go To dialogue box will help you to get where you're going more quickly.

1 When you want to go to a specific location, click the Home tab.

2 Click Find & Select, and then click Go To.

3 Select the location or type a cell address for your destination.

4 Click OK.

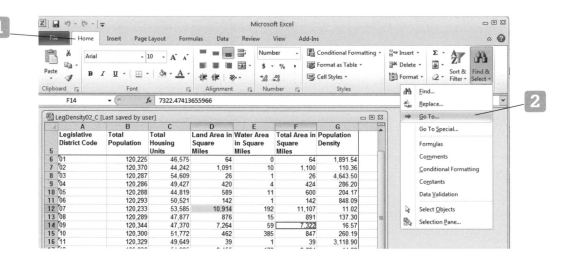

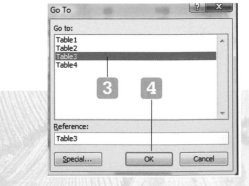

> **?** **DID YOU KNOW?**
>
> If you want to go to comments, the last cell, an object, a formula or another destination not listed in the Go To dialogue box, click Special, select a location and click OK.

Create labels

Labels are essential for understanding the data in a worksheet. They describe the information contained in rows, columns or individual cells. You don't necessarily have to create a text label; you can use a number as a label as well. The AutoComplete feature available with Excel and other Office applications helps you keep your labels consistent; it enters values based on previously entered labels.

1 Click the cell where you want to enter a label.

2 Type the content for your label.

3 Press Enter.

4 To add a number as a label, begin by typing an apostrophe (').

5 Type the number.

6 Press Enter.

| File | Home | Insert | Page Layout | Formulas | Data | Review | View | Add-Ins |

	A	B	C	D	E	F	G
44	39	120,298	46,640	4,384	54	4,439	27.44
45	40	120,279	53,343	440	605	1,045	273.39
46	41	120,289	50,301	59	10	69	2,037.21
47	42	120,300	54,405	1,142	318	1,461	105.33
48	43	120,256	65,667	11	3	15	10,517.18
49	44	120,283	43,262	102	3	105	1,178.70
50	45	120,360	45,808	236	5	241	510.04
51	46	120,267	56,476	19	6	25	6,435.91
52	47	120,302	43,689	87	2	89	1,375.62
53	48	120,294	54,101	35	10	44	3,459.98
54	49	120,467	51,285	49	10	59	2,471.36
55	Grand Total	5,894,141	2,451,081	66,544	4,756	71,300	88.58

A54 ... ✗ ✓ ƒx '49

LegDensity02_C [Last saved by user]

? DID YOU KNOW?

The apostrophe is a label prefix; it will not appear on your worksheet.

? DID YOU KNOW?

A label can contain uppercase and lowercase characters, spaces, punctuation and numbers.

Enter values on a worksheet

Entering values in worksheet cells is one of the basic tasks associated with spreadsheets. Values can take the form of whole numbers, decimals, percentages or dates. You can enter numeric values either by using the number keys at the top of your keyboard or by pressing the Num Lock key.

1 Click the cell where you want to enter a value.

2 Type the value.

3 Press Enter.

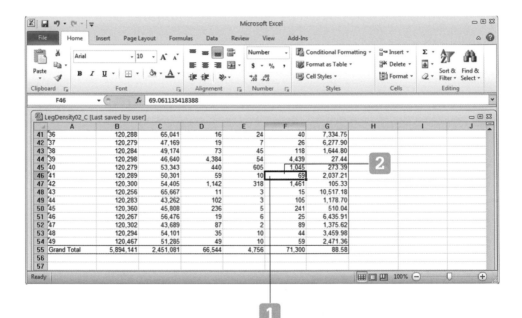

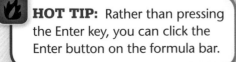

DID YOU KNOW?

When you begin to enter a date or time, Excel recognises the entries (if they correspond to one of its built-in date or time formats) and changes the information to fit its default date or time format.

Edit cell contents

One of the best things about Excel spreadsheets is the fact that they can be quickly updated. Making changes to cells is easy. But the process differs slightly from that used to enter data.

1 Double-click the cell you want to edit. The insertion point appears within the cell, and the status bar displays Edit instead of Ready.

2 If you need to move the insertion point inside the cell, use the arrow, Home or End keys.

3 Press Backspace or the Delete (Del) key, or click Clear and choose Clear All, to remove characters as needed, and type in new ones.

4 Do one of the following to end editing:

- Press Enter.

- Press the Esc key.

The status bar changes back to Ready instead of Edit.

HOT TIP: A number of shortcut key commands are available to help you streamline the editing of cell contents. You must be on the Excel 2010 Home tab to access them. Press Alt+C to copy the selected cell contents, press Alt+V to paste them and press Alt+FP to display the Format Painter so you can copy formatting from one cell to another.

Clear cell contents

When you first start using Excel, you might think clearing a cell's contents is a simple matter of pressing the Backspace or Delete key. But Excel 2007 gives you control over exactly what you want to clear. In case you have applied formatting to a cell and you want to keep the formatting even as you cut the data, Excel lets you do it.

1 Click to select the cell or range of cells you want to clear.

2 Click the Home tab if necessary.

3 Click the Clear button, and choose one of the following:

- Clear All to clear both contents and formatting.

- Clear Formats to clear formatting but leave contents.

- Clear Contents to clear contents and leave formatting.

- Clear Comments to clear comments you have made to cells.

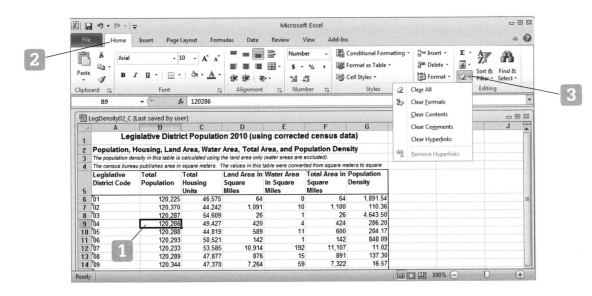

HOT TIP: To clear contents more quickly, right-click the contents and choose Clear Contents from the context menu.

Select rows, columns and special ranges

By now, you know how to select a single cell or a range of cells – or even a non-contiguous set of cells. Sometimes, when working with Excel, you'll need to select entire rows or columns, entire worksheets, or ranges that span multiple worksheets. If the need arises, try the techniques described in this section.

1 To select an entire row or column, click to select a cell anywhere in the column, and press Shift+space bar.

2 After you select an entire row or column, if you need to select other, non-adjacent rows or columns, press and hold down Ctrl while you click anywhere in the borders for the other columns you want.

? DID YOU KNOW?

If you have selected an entire row or column and you need to select adjacent rows or columns, drag over the adjacent row or column headings.

3 To select a multisheet range, select the range in one sheet.

4 Select the worksheet tabs at the bottom of the Excel window to choose the worksheets you want to include in the same range.

SEE ALSO: See the section Select cells at the beginning of this chapter for some tips on selecting groups of cells.

Name a worksheet

Each Excel workbook opens with three worksheets in which you can work with information. The default worksheet names are the generic designations Sheet1, Sheet2 and Sheet3. Whenever you need to add a worksheet, you click the Insert Worksheet tab at the bottom of the window. You can then name your new worksheet – or change the generic names of other sheets to more recognisable ones – with just a few steps.

1 To select a worksheet, click one of these tabs.

2 To add a new worksheet, click the Insert Worksheet tab.

3 To name a worksheet, double-click its sheet tab.

4 Type a new name.

5 Press Enter.

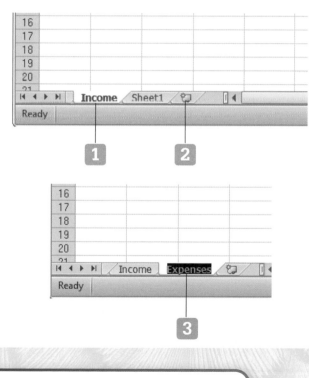

HOT TIP: To select all worksheets at once, right-click any sheet tab and choose Select All Sheets.

Delete a worksheet

Sometimes, you end up with more worksheet space than you have information. To keep the file size small and your workbooks manageable, delete any unneeded sheets.

1 Click the tab of the sheet you want to remove.

2 Click the Home tab, if necessary.

3 Click the Delete button down arrow and choose Delete Sheet.

4 Click Delete to confirm the operation.

HOT TIP: You can also right-click the sheet tab and choose Delete from the context menu to quickly remove a sheet.

Move or copy a worksheet

After you assemble your data, you might need to reorder worksheets to fit a particular pattern – to put them in chronological order, for instance. You can either copy the worksheet to the new location and then delete the previous version, or simply move the sheet from one place to another. In either case, Excel 2010 makes the task easy.

1 Click the sheet tab of the worksheet you want to copy.

2 Click the Home tab.

3 Click the Format button down arrow and choose Move or Copy Sheet.

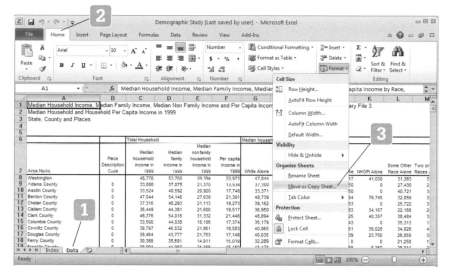

4 To copy the sheet to another workbook you have open, click the To book drop-down list and choose the name of the workbook.

5 To copy the sheet to another location in the current workbook, choose another sheet from the list.

6 Click OK.

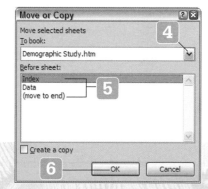

? DID YOU KNOW?

When you copy the sheet to another location in the same workbook, Excel places it to the left of (or before) the sheet you choose.

🔥 HOT TIP: To quickly copy a worksheet, press and hold down the Ctrl key while you drag the sheet's name to another location in the worksheet tabs.

Insert a column or row

When you add a new blank column or row to a worksheet, Excel preserves existing columns and rows as well as any formulas that apply to them. However, formulas that make absolute (rather than relative) references to cells will need to be adjusted manually. When you insert a column, it is placed to the left of the column you select. When you insert a row, it goes above the row you select.

1 Click anywhere to the right of the new column you want to add, or immediately below the row you want to add.

2 Click the Home tab.

3 Click the Insert down arrow, and choose Insert Sheet Columns or Insert Sheet Rows.

4 If you need to adjust formatting, click the Insert Options button and choose a formatting option.

? DID YOU KNOW?

You can insert more than one column or row at a time. First, drag to select the row header buttons or column header buttons that correspond to the number of columns or rows you want to add. If you want to insert two rows above row 18, select row 18 and 19, for instance. Then click Insert and choose Insert Sheet Columns or Insert Sheet Rows as needed.

Delete a column or row

In the course of editing data, you may need to remove a whole row or column rather than a cell or group of cells. The process is similar to that for inserting rows or columns. The remaining columns will be moved either to the left or up to join the rest of the data.

1 Select the header button of the column or row you want to delete.

2 Click the Home tab.

3 Click the Delete button and then choose Delete Sheet Columns or Delete Sheet Rows.

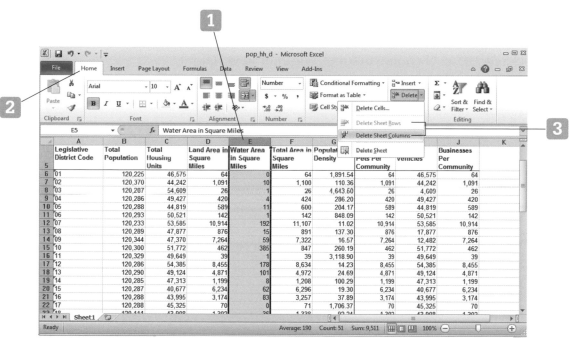

<table>
<tr><td>! ALERT:</td></tr>
</table>

> **!** **ALERT:** Make sure you check formulas in your worksheet before you delete the row or column. You might not want to delete formulas that make absolute references to the cells you are about to delete.

> **?** **DID YOU KNOW?**
> You can select multiple header buttons for columns or rows if you need to delete multiple items.

Adjust column or row size

Once you have entered data in your worksheet, you'll probably need to do some formatting. Adjusting the width of columns and the height of rows makes your information more readable, especially if some of your data isn't visible in its entirety. It also happens that the labels turn out larger than the width of a column, and you need to widen the columns to make them visible. You can easily change the default size of both rows and columns to accommodate your labels and data.

1 Click the column or row header of the column or row you need to adjust.

2 Optionally, you can select more columns or rows if you need to adjust them at once.

3 Click the Home tab if needed.

4 Click Format, and choose Column Width or Row Height.

5 Type the new column width or row height in points.

6 Click OK.

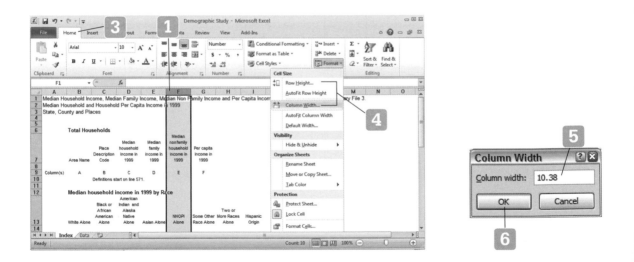

HOT TIP: You can also right-click the selected column or row and choose Column Width or Row Height from the context menu.

DID YOU KNOW?
One centimetre equals 28.8 points.

Divide a worksheet into panes

If you are working with a worksheet that contains many computer screens' worth of data, you can't see the entire contents at once. Rather than having to scroll up and down between different parts of the file, you can divide it into four panes. That way you can scroll independently through each of the two parts of the worksheet and work with both parts at once.

1 Click a cell, column or row to select the area of the file where you want to create separate panes.

2 Click the View tab.

3 Click Split.

4 If you want to remove the split and return to one pane, click the Split button again.

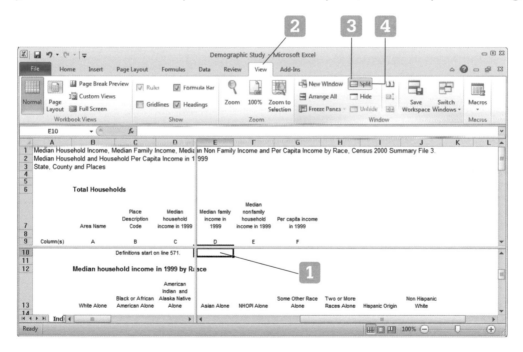

? DID YOU KNOW?

If you select a cell, you split the worksheet into four panes. If you select a row or column, you divide it in two.

? DID YOU KNOW?

Once you have two panes, you can resize them by dragging the drag bar at the bottom right-hand corner of the Excel window or by clicking and dragging the pane divider up and down.

Create a basic formula

Formulas are powerful features of Excel worksheets. They calculate values you have entered and return results for you. Excel provides you with a set of operators that you can use to perform addition, multiplication, division and other calculations. Each formula starts with an argument: the cell references or values that combine to produce a result. If your formula gets too long, you can resize the formula bar to accommodate it.

1 Click the cell that you want to contain the formula.

2 Type the equals sign (=) to begin so Excel will calculate the values you enter. (If you don't, Excel will simply display what you type.)

2 **4**

=B20*E18

3 **5**

3 Enter the first argument – a number or a cell reference.

4 Enter an operator such as the asterisk (*) for multiplication.

5 Enter the next argument and repeat values and operators as needed.

6 Press Enter or click the Enter button on the formula bar. The result appears in the cell.

? **DID YOU KNOW?**
By default, only formula results are displayed in a cell, but you can adjust the worksheet view to display the formula itself.

HOT TIP: Point to a cell rather than typing its address so you reduce the chance of typing errors.

6 **Formula bar**

Display formulas

By default, formulas aren't displayed in your worksheet cells. When you press Enter or click the Enter button on the formula bar, the calculation you have specified is performed. You may want to display formulas in the cells rather than automatically calculating them, however. Do so by following these steps:

1 Click the Formulas tab.

2 Click Show Formulas.

3 Click the Show Formulas button again to disable formula display.

	F	G	H	I
11	142.496238206509	848.090818406833		
12	11106.914757134	11.0159143511641		
13	891.391650077142	137.295169084094		
14	7322.47413655966	16.5676120232317		
15	847.460353870366	260.189228876937		
16	39.1250079150945	3118.90310090662		
17	8633.51288770448	14.2265385732088		
18	4972.15603856078	24.6948600524287		
19	1207.55912035114	100.292407410965		
20	6296.34875682821	19.2955862478241		
21	3256.89290606752	37.894532486135		
22	70.8459193633328	1706.37374588754		=B40+C40
23	1337.68451398231	92.2390814057775		
24	2163.70918359467	67.7765332201994		
25	2785.69591287681	43.6766787397265		
26	53.6008495020054	3706.49641484833		

Cell: I22, fx =B40+C40

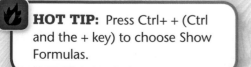

HOT TIP: Press Ctrl+ + (Ctrl and the + key) to choose Show Formulas.

Use Formula AutoComplete

One of Excel 2010's most useful new features is Formula AutoComplete. It provides you with suggestions of valid functions, arguments, defined names and other items that help you accurately complete a formula without typing everything from scratch. Whenever you type a text string, a drop-down list appears with items that will help you complete your typing.

1 Click the cell where you want to enter the formula.

2 Type = (the equals sign) and some beginning letters of a formula to start Formula AutoComplete.

3 Scan the list of valid items, which changes as you type.

4 Press Tab or double-click an item to select it.

Edit a formula

It's not difficult to edit a formula, especially since the formula bar just above your worksheet data is available for this purpose. But there are a couple of tricks you need to perform in order to enter Edit mode and make the necessary changes.

1 Select the cell that contains the formula you need to edit.

2 Press F2 to enter Edit mode.

3 Use the Home, End and arrow keys on your computer keyboard to move through the formula so you can make edits.

4 Press Backspace or Del (Delete) to remove items so you can make corrections.

5 When you've finished, click Enter on the formula bar or press Enter.

HOT TIP: Excel 2010 makes it easy to correct errors in formulas. Click the Formula tab. Click Formula Auditing and then click Error Checking. When the Error Checking dialogue box appears, it will display any errors. Click Fix in the formula bar to correct them.

Apply conditional formatting

Conditional formatting gives you a way to indicate a cell's value by displaying special formatting. For example, you can have a numeral less than zero be displayed in red. You can have especially high sales figures be highlighted in green and bold. The formatting is used only if the value meets the criteria you specify.

1 Select the cell or range of cells you want to format using conditions you specify.

2 Click the Home tab if necessary.

3 Click Conditional Formatting, and point to Highlight Cells Rules.

4 Click a rule you want to specify as part of your conditional formatting.

5 Enter the criteria you want.

6 Click OK.

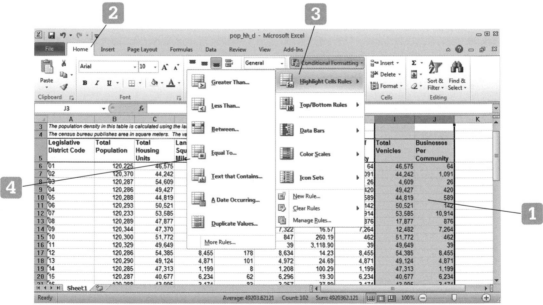

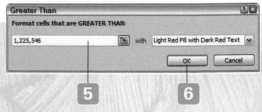

? DID YOU KNOW?

You can only apply conditional formatting to cells that contain text, number, or date or time values.

7 Assembling PowerPoint presentations

Introduction

PowerPoint presentations need to look good. The purpose of such presentations is that you are going to share them with others – often, in a classroom or a business environment. You need to take care with how your words and images appear, and, fortunately for you, PowerPoint 2010 gives you the tools to do this. These include lists, images, charts, tables and multimedia clips. You can move objects freely from one part of a presentation to another as you assemble your work.

Like other Office 2010 applications, PowerPoint provides an AutoCorrect feature that minimises typographical errors. A built-in thesaurus and dictionary help you choose the right words. And an outline pane gives you a place to make notes that will help you edit your presentation at a later date. The 2010 version of PowerPoint is more stable than previous versions, and it adds the capacity to group slides into sections. This enables you to hide or view groups of slides all at once.

After you gather the words and images and arrange them on slides, you need to consider how best to present them. You'll find PowerPoint 2010's navigation tools helpful when moving around your presentation. As you make the presentation, you can use your mouse as a pointer. You can also add notes to your slide show to highlight important points for your viewers. You can also store your presentation as a compressed file or save it on CD-ROM so you can use it any time you wish.

Navigate a presentation

PowerPoint presentations give you a number of shortcuts you can use to find your way around a presentation quickly. In addition, some buttons in the PowerPoint window perform special functions that can be time savers.

1 Click the Up or Down arrows to scroll line by line.

2 Click the Previous Slide and Next Slide buttons to move one slide at a time.

3 Click one of the thumbnails in the Slides pane to jump to that slide.

4 Use this scroll bar to view the thumbnails quickly.

HOT TIP: Press the PgUp or PgDn buttons to move between slides one at a time.

Switch views

PowerPoint, like Word and Excel, gives you different ways of viewing information. The default view is just one of several options. Take a moment to browse through the other options so you know what's available. When it comes time to put the finishing touches on your slide show you'll be happy to use Slide Sorter or Slide Show View, for instance.

1 To switch from one view to another, do one of the following:

- Click the View tab and click one of the options in the Presentation Views group.
- Click one of the view buttons in the status bar.

2 The available options are:

- Normal View: contains the outline, slide, and notes in their own panes.
- Slide Sorter: displays slides in sections and provides transitions.
- Slide Show: this view displays your slides one at a time.
- Reading View: displays one slide in its own screen.

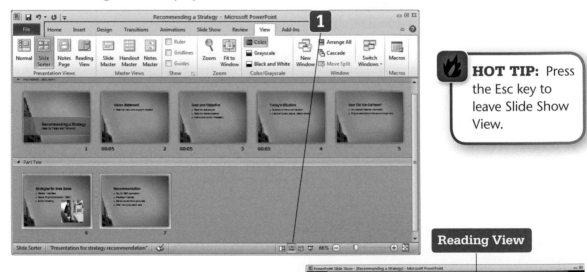

HOT TIP: Press the Esc key to leave Slide Show View.

Reading View

HOT TIP: Slide Sorter View is one of two views (Normal is the other) that enables you to group slides into sections, a new feature in Office 2010. Slide Sorter View is especially useful for viewing and creating sections.

Create a new slide

Whether you want to create a new blank slide or apply an existing slide's formatting to a new one, PowerPoint makes it easy to do so. The tools are especially effective when it comes to creating a consistent appearance throughout a presentation. Any slide layout contains placeholders for images, text, charts and other objects.

1 Click the Home tab if needed.

2 Click the down arrow next to New Slide.

3 Choose the layout you want from the Slide Layout gallery.

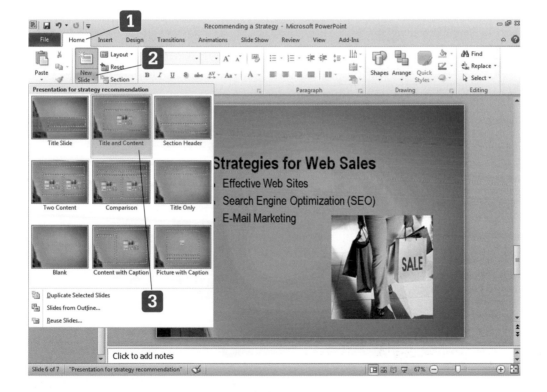

HOT TIP: If you want to add a blank slide quickly, click the Add Slide button.

Change a slide's layout

Once you insert a slide, you can apply one of a group of predetermined layouts to it. The layouts have colour, type and the general arrangement already set. You can also apply a custom layout you prepare yourself.

1 Make sure you are in Normal view.

2 Click the Home tab.

3 Click the Layout button, and choose the layout you want.

Work with objects

Once you add a text block, image, chart or other object to a slide, you can easily move, copy or resize it. Before you perform any action on an object, you first need to select it. An object that has been selected is outlined by a rectangle called a selection box that has sizing handles at the corner.

1 Select an object by moving the pointer over it and clicking it.

2 Move the object by hovering the pointer over it (it becomes a four-headed arrow) and dragging with the mouse.

3 To resize the object, click and drag one of the sizing handles; to constrain the original shape, press Shift while you drag.

4 To select the object, click anywhere outside its boundaries.

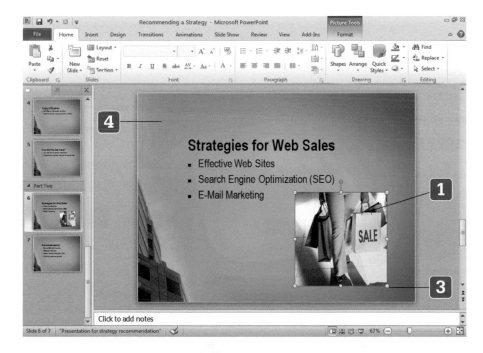

? DID YOU KNOW?

To copy the object, press and hold down the Ctrl key while dragging.

? DID YOU KNOW?

When your pointer is over an object and it can be clicked, the pointer changes to a four-headed arrow.

Insert a template

If you don't want to create a presentation from scratch, turn to the templates that Office 2010 provides. PowerPoint comes with a selection of installed templates. If you don't find the one you want, you'll find a wide selection at Microsoft Office Online. You can choose everything from invitations to agendas. By starting with a template, you get a suggested set of slides that you can modify to fit your own needs.

1 Click the File tab.

2 Click New.

3 Click one of the options in the categories of templates that either came with PowerPoint or that you can access at Office Online.

4 Select the template you want.

5 Click Create.

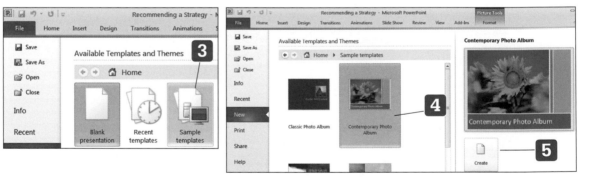

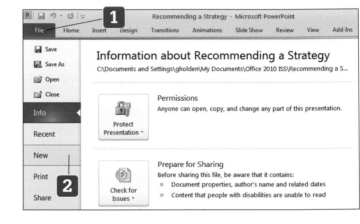

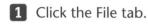

! ALERT: Some of the templates on Office Online were submitted by individuals rather than Microsoft itself. Make sure there aren't any permissions issues before you copy a template.

? DID YOU KNOW?

To download the Microsoft Office Online templates, you need to use Internet Explorer rather than another browser; an Active X control may have to be installed so you can view and install the template you want.

Use text placeholders

If you're used to entering text in Word or even in an Excel worksheet, you're used to simply positioning the cursor and typing. In PowerPoint, text is treated as an object like images and charts. When you insert one of PowerPoint's templates, text is provided in a box with a dashed line around it – a placeholder – that you can replace with your own content.

1 Make sure you are in Normal view.

2 Click the text placeholder once to select it.

3 Type the text you want to enter.

4 Click anywhere outside the text box to deselect it.

HOT TIP: Once you insert a placeholder, you can resize it by clicking it once and then dragging the borders around it.

Select and modify text

After you create text in PowerPoint, it is contained in a box with sizing handles, just like an image. This makes it easy to move and modify text as well as enter it.

1 Click once to select the placeholder.

2 Click inside the placeholder to position the insertion point.

3 Double-click to select a word; press Backspace or Del to delete text so you can type new content.

4 Click anywhere outside the box to deselect it.

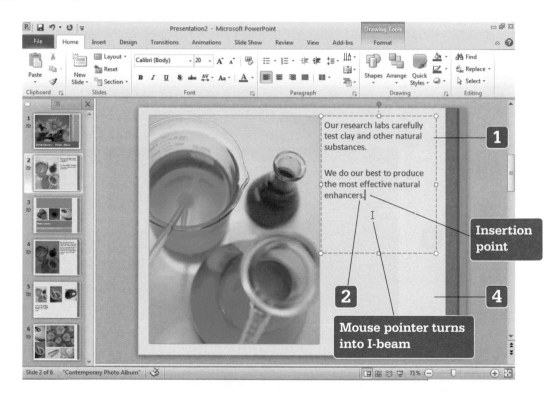

Create a list

Bulleted and numbered lists are important parts of nearly every PowerPoint presentation. They present information in a compact way and give the presenter a natural set of 'talking points' that can be covered while giving a talk about a subject.

1 Make sure you are in Normal view, and click the Home tab.

2 Position the text cursor at the point where you want the list to begin.

3 Click the Bulleted or Numbered List button.

4 Type the first list item, and then press Enter.

5 Type the second item.

6 Repeat steps 4 and 5 until the list is complete.

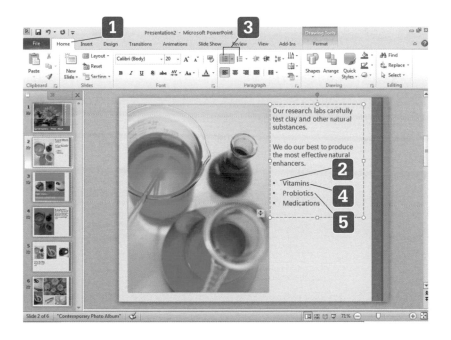

? DID YOU KNOW?
You can increase the list level, press the Tab key or click the Increase List Level button on the Home tab. To decrease the level, press Shift+Tab or click the Decrease List Level button on the Home tab.

HOT TIP: Make sure you press the space bar once to separate the bullet or number from the item that follows it.

Take advantage of AutoFit

One of the nice features of PowerPoint 2007 is the ability to automatically fit text to the size of the available text box. This maximises the visibility of text on a screen when you are giving a presentation. AutoFit means you don't have to change the size manually.

1 To turn on AutoFit, click the File tab.

2 Choose Options.

3 Click Proofing.

4 Click AutoCorrect Options.

5 Click the AutoFormat As You Type tab.

6 Tick the AutoFit title next to placeholder and AutoFit body text to placeholder check boxes.

7 Click OK.

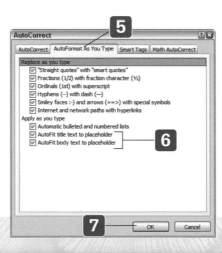

? DID YOU KNOW?

If you don't like the AutoFit feature (it takes some time to get used to it) and you want to turn it off, use the AutoFit dialogue box to do so: untick the AutoFit title text to placeholder and AutoFit body text to placeholder check boxes.

Develop an outline

Outlines are useful not only for organising your thoughts but for giving a presentation as well. You can easily develop your own outline from scratch in the Outline Pane or insert one from a presentation or document you have already made.

1 Click the Outline tab in the navigation pane to switch to Outline View.

2 Click in the outline pane to position the cursor where you want the outline to appear.

3 Type the outline title and press Enter.

4 To indent the next item to the right a level, press Tab before typing.

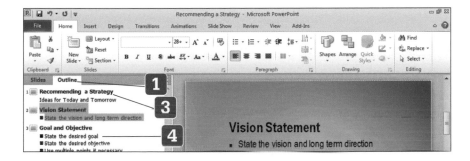

5 When you want to insert a slide in the outline pane click the New Slide button and then choose a layout.

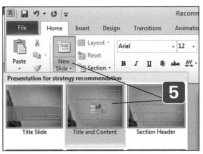

HOT TIP: Press Shift+Tab to demote an item a level.

? DID YOU KNOW?

You can insert an outline you created from another Office application such as Word. Click the New Slide down arrow, choose Slides from Outline, locate the outline file and click Insert.

Duplicate a slide

When you are creating a presentation or editing one, you don't need to begin every slide from scratch. If you have a slide with the layout and type and colour configuration you want, you can duplicate it with a few mouse clicks.

1 In Normal view, click the slide you want to duplicate in the Outline pane.

2 Click the Home tab.

3 Click the New Slide down arrow.

4 Click Duplicate Selected Slides.

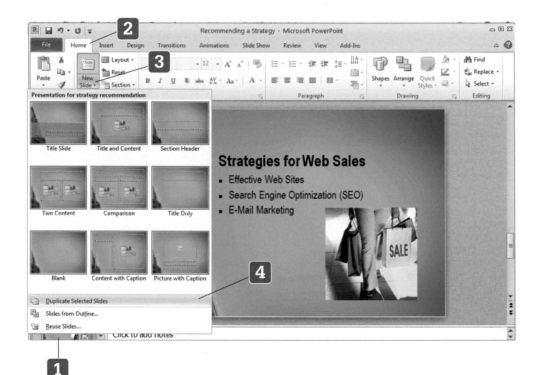

Manage slides with the Slide Sorter

Slide Sorter View gives you an effective way to get an overview of all the slides in a presentation. You can use this view to rearrange slides by dragging and dropping them.

1 Click the View tab.

2 Click the Slide Sorter button.

3 Click the slide you want to move and hold down the mouse button.

4 Drag the slide to a new location.

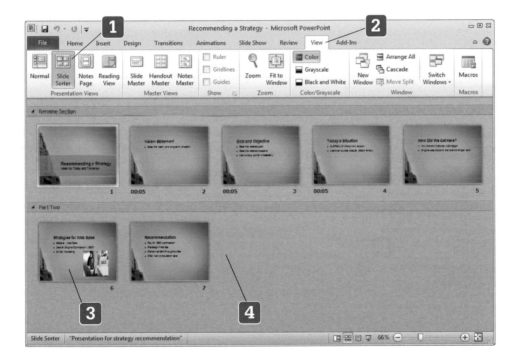

? DID YOU KNOW?

A vertical line appears where the slide will be moved when you release the mouse button.

▶ SEE ALSO: See the section Switch views earlier in this chapter for more on Slide Sorter View.

Import slides

You can bring slides into the presentation you're assembling either by copying and pasting them or by using a new feature called the Reuse Slides task pane. The advantage of the Reuse Slides task pane is that you don't have to have the previous presentation (the one from which you are taking the slides) open first.

1 Click the Home tab if necessary.

2 Click the New Slide down arrow and choose Reuse Slides.

3 In the Reuse Slides task pane, click Browse, choose Browse File, select the file you want and click Open.

4 Select the slide you want to import.

5 Click Close to close the task pane.

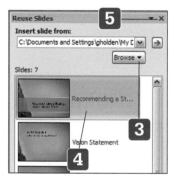

HOT TIP: To insert all slides at once, right-click any slide and choose Insert All Slides.

Insert a slide master

A slide master is a container for objects such as logos or text-based slogans that you want to appear on each slide in your presentation. The slide master includes controls that let you delete, rename or copy masters. You can lock a master to keep it from being deleted.

1 Click the View tab.

2 Click the Slide Master button.

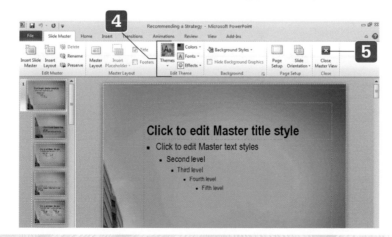

3 Click the Insert tab to add objects, or type text on the master.

4 On the Slide Master tab, Click Colors, Themes, Fonts or other controls to edit the theme of the master slide.

5 When you're done, click the Close Master View button.

? DID YOU KNOW?

When you insert a slide master, it is added just beneath the currently displayed slide.

Insert placeholder content

Slide masters include a set of layouts that you can choose. In order to customise the layout, you can add content in the form of placeholders. You can add content, text, picture, chart, table, diagram, media or Clip Art placeholders. The content will then appear on each slide in your presentation.

1 Click View and choose Slide Master to open the Slide Master tab.

2 Choose the slide master in the left pane.

3 Click the Insert Layout button to associate a new layout with the slide master.

4 Click the down arrow next to Insert Placeholder and click the type of placeholder you want to add.

5 Click and drag to create a placeholder on the slide layout.

6 When you're done, click the Close Master View button.

? **DID YOU KNOW?**

You can simply click the Insert Placeholder button rather than clicking the down arrow. This adds a generic placeholder that can hold any kind of content.

Change the page setup

If you ever need to print out a presentation, you need to first make sure it will appear the way you want. By default, PowerPoint uses landscape orientation and starts slides at number one. To check the overall printed page size and the orientation of each page, open the Page Setup dialogue box.

1 Click the Design tab.

2 Click Page Setup.

3 Choose an option from the Slides sized for drop-down list to specify the height–width proportion for slides in your presentation.

4 Specify the width and height of each slide.

5 Choose Portrait or Landscape orientation.

6 Click OK.

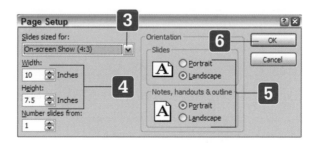

? DID YOU KNOW?

If you want to change the number at which your slides start, enter a number other than one in the Number slides from box.

! ALERT: The Design tab does not appear if the Slide Master tab is open. Close the Slide Master tab if necessary.

Adjust slide timing

When you play a presentation as a slide show, it's important to adjust the timing between slides to make sure the presentation goes by at the optimal speed.

1 Click the Slide Show tab.

2 Click the Rehearse Timings button.

3 As the time goes by in the Rehearsal dialogue box, press Enter to move from one slide to the next.

4 When you have finished and a confirmation dialogue box appears, click Yes to accept the timings.

Edit slide timing

If you need to change the timing between slides, you can use the Animations tab, one of several new tabs that are available in Slide Sorter View.

1 To edit timings, switch to Slide Sorter View.

2 Click the slide or slides whose timings you want to change.

3 Click the Transitions tab.

4 Type a new value in the Duration box.

5 Press Enter to save the new timing.

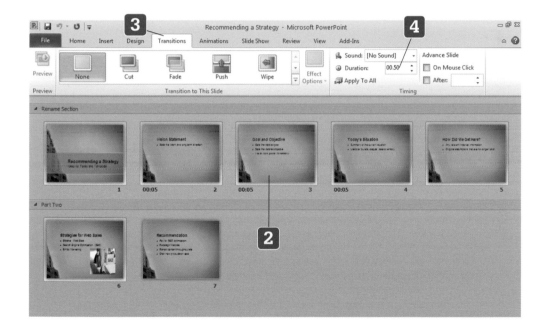

? DID YOU KNOW?
The Transitions tab is new to Office 2010.

HOT TIP: To switch to Slide Sorter View, click the View tab and then click Slide Sorter.

8 Creating an Access database

Introduction

Many of the Office 2010 applications discussed in preceding chapters help you organise information, but nothing allows you to organise the way Access 2010 does. Access has the capacity to store huge amounts of data in a highly organised database structure that makes it easy to find and retrieve information. You can also create forms that allow you to enter information in a database.

You don't need to be highly experienced with databases to use Access, either. Like other Office 2010 applications, Access comes with templates you can use for personal, business or other purposes. And if you want to edit a database created in an earlier version of Access or other programs, you'll find it easy to do so. And this new version of Access makes it easier than ever to format content for the Web so that others can access information with their web browsers.

This chapter introduces you to some of the many basic database functions you can perform with Access. You don't need to master complex database design to start working with data. You'll learn how to create a database, view data, enter new data and print out reports that help you and your colleagues interpret the information you've assembled.

Use a template to create a database

The simplest way to create an Access database is to use one of the templates that come with the application. Templates contain all the elements you need to organise data, including fields, tables, queries, reports and forms.

1 Click the File tab.

2 Choose New. You switch to Microsoft Access 2010 Backstage View.

3 Click the type of template you want to use in the Available Templates pane. You can search through templates installed with Access or, if you are connected to the Internet, those provided at Microsoft Office Online.

4 Click the specific template you want.

5 Click the Browse button, click the Save in down arrow and save the file on your computer.

6 Click Create.

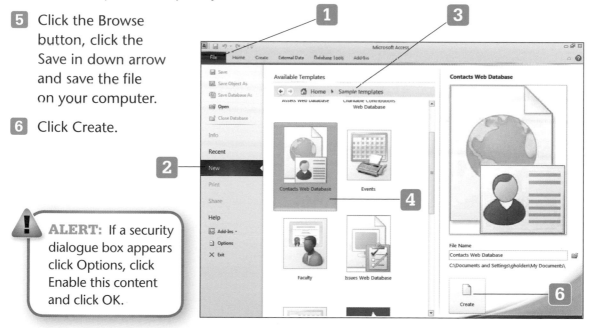

! ALERT: If a security dialogue box appears click Options, click Enable this content and click OK.

? DID YOU KNOW?

An Access database consists of several different elements, including: forms – let you enter information into a database; tables – contain a set of data about a topic, each contained in a separate field; queries – give you a way to locate information stored in a database; reports – summaries of the data stored in a database; macros – programs that provide a single shortcut for a series of actions you need to perform; and modules – programs that extend the functionality of a database.

Assemble a blank database

If Access's templates don't cover your needs or if you need to create a custom database, you can quickly create one from scratch. You just need to name your file and save it in a location where you can find it easily.

1 Click the File tab.

2 Click New.

3 Click Blank Database.

4 If necessary, click the Browse button, click the Save in down arrow and click OK to choose a location for your file.

5 Type a name for your file and click Create.

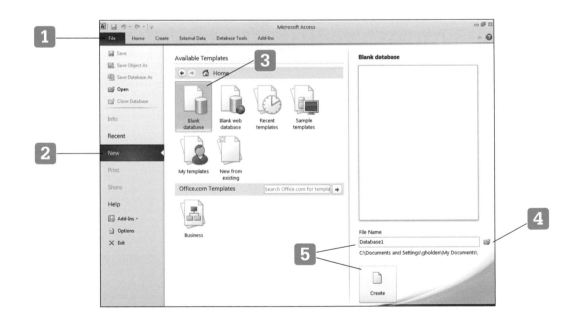

Work with the Access window

Once you create a new database, you need to start working with the parts of the Access window that help you to manipulate and store data. Access 2010 presents you with the same ribbon-based interface you see in other Office 2010 applications, but it also includes a set of tabs that display tables, queries, forms, reports and macros. The navigation pane shows you the database objects you currently have.

1 Click the Save button in the quick access toolbar periodically to save your work.

2 Click the double arrows to display or hide the navigation pane.

3 Click the tabs to view the objects you can work with in the currently open database.

4 Click one of the View buttons to move from one view to another:

- Form View
- Datasheet View
- Layout View
- Design View

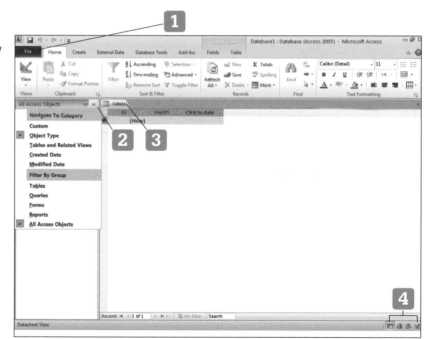

Customise Access display options

You can change what appears in the Access window by customising the program's display options. Not only that, but you can customise the options that appear in a specific database. You can also display the form you want to appear on startup.

1 Click the File tab and click Options.

2 Click Current Database in the left-hand pane.

3 Enter a database application title.

4 Choose the form object you want to display on startup.

5 Tick the display options you want or untick the ones you don't.

6 Click OK.

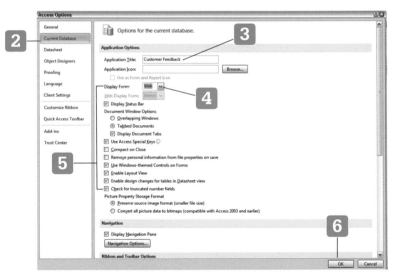

? DID YOU KNOW?

Access Options let you display your database objects as a set of tabbed documents that you can easily access, or as overlapping windows.

? DID YOU KNOW?

A feature new to Access 2010, Layout View, lets you change the design of a form or report while you view it.

Add fields to a blank database

Even if you choose to create a blank database file from scratch, Access is there to provide help if you need it. A generic Add New Field object is added and highlighted so you can replace it with a specific type of field. When the database opens, a set of commonly used field templates is provided for you. A field template is a predesigned field with a name, data type, length and other preset properties. You can choose the templates and add them to your file, or create your own generic fields.

1 To create a blank field, click the down arrow next to Click to Add.

2 If you need a specific type of field, scroll down the list and click one that fits your needs.

3 If you need more fields, click the Fields tab and click More Fields.

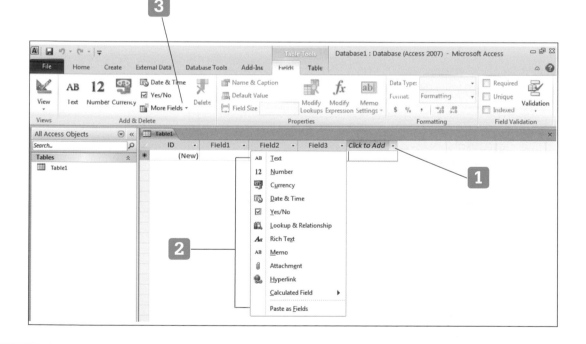

? **DID YOU KNOW?**

Open the navigation pane and choose a table to which you want to add a field. When you open a table the Table Tools tab appears in the ribbon. Click the Datasheet tab to view the Field Templates.

? **DID YOU KNOW?**

When you add a field to the datasheet, position it between the headers of existing fields by clicking the field that you want to appear next to the new one.

Reuse existing fields

If you are working with a template or with an existing database, you will probably want to reuse fields that already exist in the file. Access 2010 makes it easy to do so; just choose one of the existing fields from the field list and drag it into the datasheet to use it. But you need to be in Design View to access the field list.

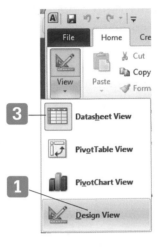

1 Switch to Design View, if necessary, by clicking the Home tab, clicking the Views button and then choosing Design View from the drop-down list.

2 Right-click the field you want to use and choose Copy from the context menu.

3 Return to Datasheet View.

4 Right-click the spot in the table where you want to reuse the field and choose Paste from the context menu.

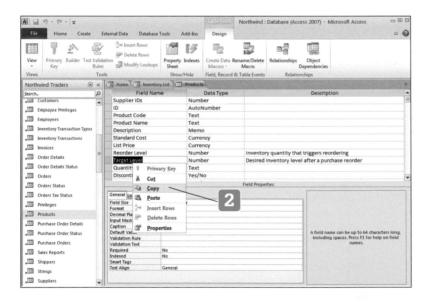

? DID YOU KNOW?
Specific types of fields, such as the Total Row, let you perform calculations such as sum, count, average, or maximum or minimum.

HOT TIP: You need to close all open objects in order to switch from Datasheet View or another view to Design View. If objects are open, you'll be prompted to close them first.

Explore database objects

Every Access database contains up to seven different types of objects. Each object, together with the others, constitutes a complete picture of the data you have stored. You locate and move between the different database objects in the navigation pane on the left-hand side of the Access window. The navigation pane also includes a drop-down list. The drop-down list also lets you view database contents by categories and groups. Click the down arrow at the top of the navigation pane, and you can view predefined and custom categories for the currently open database: the upper section lists the categories and the lower section lists predefined and custom groups for the categories.

1 Open the database file you want to work with.

2 Click the Open/Close button to open the navigation pane fully, if needed.

3 Double-click the button for the object you want to view.

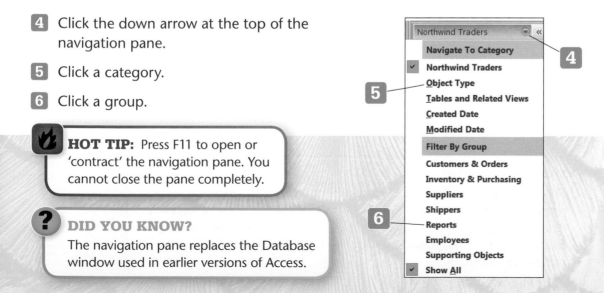

4 Click the down arrow at the top of the navigation pane.

5 Click a category.

6 Click a group.

HOT TIP: Press F11 to open or 'contract' the navigation pane. You cannot close the pane completely.

? DID YOU KNOW?
The navigation pane replaces the Database window used in earlier versions of Access.

Manage database objects

The objects that make up a database are there to help you track and work with your data. But you don't have to stick with the default names of these objects. You can create new objects, hide some objects or delete them. That way, each database will only have the selection of objects you need.

1 Double-click an object in the navigation pane to open it, or right-click the object to change its design.

2 Choose Delete from the context menu to delete the object.

3 Click the Create tab.

4 Click the button for the type of object you want to create.

5 Work with the object when it opens in the reading pane.

6 Click the object's Close button when you are finished.

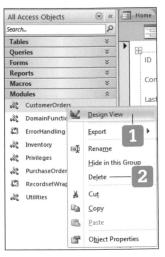

Create an application part

The objects that make up a database are there to help you track and work with your data. But you don't have to stick the default names of objects. You can create new objects, hide some objects, or delete them. That way, each database will have only the selection of objects you need. You can also access prebuilt application parts – objects that either come with Access or that others have saved for reuse in your organisation. Using prebuilt application parts saves time and helps an organisation achieve consistency as well.

1 Double-click an object in the navigation pane to open it, or right-click the object to change its design.

2 Click the Create tab.

3 Click Application Parts in the Templates section of the tab.

4 Click the application part you want to work with.

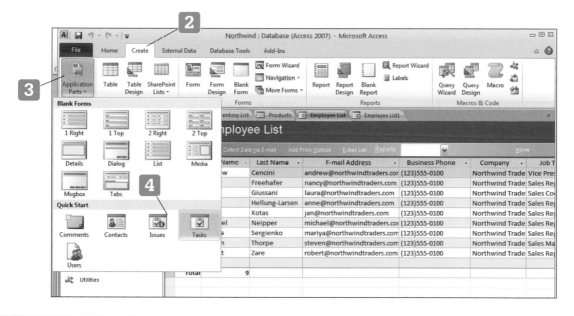

5 Create a relationship between this object and another in the database.

6 Click Next.

7 Choose the column from which the value will be obtained.

8 Click Create.

Enter and find table records

Once you create a table, you need to work with the fields within it. A field contains a type of information – an order date, a product name, a quantity. You enter the data one field at a time. A toolbar just above the status bar at the bottom of the table helps you create new records or move from one to another.

1 In the navigation pane, click the Tables object and double-click the table you want to open.

2 Click the New Record button.

3 Press Tab to accept the AutoNumber entry.

4 Type the data.

5 Press Tab to move to the next field.

6 Click a Record button. You can choose from First Record, Previous Record, Specific Record, Next Record and Last Record.

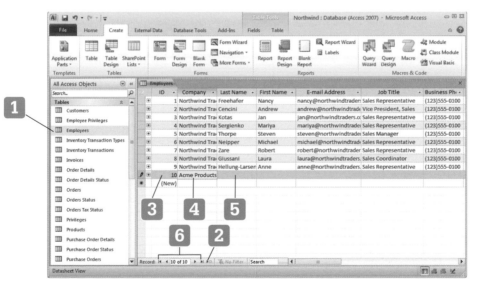

ALERT: The first field in a table is usually one called AutoNumber, which assigns a unique number to each record. You cannot select or change this field's value.

DID YOU KNOW?
Click the Table Design button to add or delete rows or columns or change other aspects of the table's design.

Find records

Tables can contain thousands of fields, and finding specific information can be difficult. The quickest option is to use Access's built-in search function.

1 Double-click the table you want to open.

2 Click Find in the Home tab.

3 In the Find and Replace dialogue box, type the text you want to find.

4 Click the Look In down arrow to select a search location.

5 Click the Match drop-down list to select the type of match you want.

6 Click Find Next.

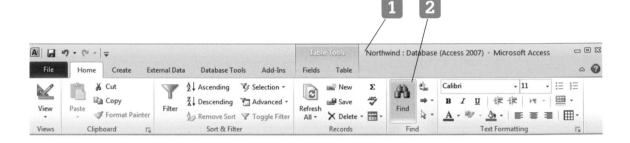

HOT TIP: If you want to search within a single field, click it before you click Find.

? DID YOU KNOW?

You can narrow your search further by choosing the Match Case check to match upper- or lowercase.

Create a database query

A query is a question that you submit to a database in order to extract the information you need. Queries are far more complex and powerful than the Find utility; they allow you to compile complex sets of data. The Query Wizard is a good place to get started with creating queries.

1 Click the Create tab.

2 Click the Query Wizard button.

> **HOT TIP:** Click Query design to design your own new query from scratch without using the wizard.

3 Click Simple Query Wizard and click OK.

4 Click the fields you want included in the query and click the right-hand arrow to move the fields to the right-hand side of the dialogue box.

5 When you've finished, click Next.

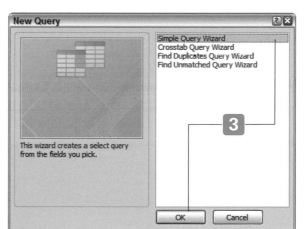

DID YOU KNOW?

If you choose a numeric or date field for the query, be sure to indicate whether you want to see details or summary information. If you choose to see a summary, click Summary Options and then click OK.

Configure and view query results

Once you compose a query, as you learned in the preceding task, you choose options for how the results will be presented. You also have the option to modify your query before you make it.

1 Enter a name for your query.

2 Select whether you want to view information from the query or modify the query.

3 Click Next (if you want to modify the query) or Finish (if you want to open the query).

4 If you chose to modify the query, you can untick fields you want to remove.

5 View results in the reading pane.

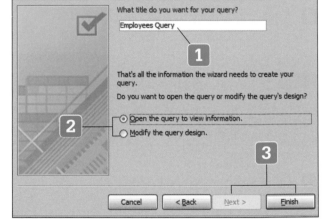

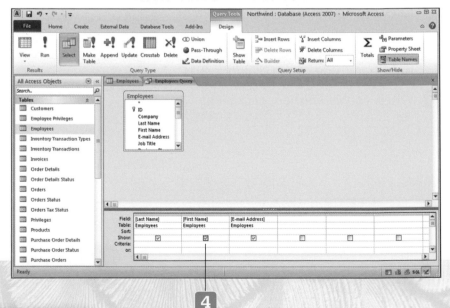

Create a form – part 1

In order to create a database, you need to enter the data. Clicking from one field to another and typing data can be time-consuming, particularly if the fields are far apart in the file – in different tables, for instance. A form gives you a user-friendly way to do data entry. Forms can enter data in multiple tables, for instance. The quickest way to create a form is to use Access's built-in Form Wizard.

1 Click the Create tab.

2 Click Form Wizard.

3 Choose a table or query on which to base your form.

4 Click the fields you want and move it to the right-hand side of the dialogue box.

5 Click Next.

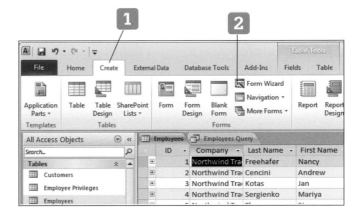

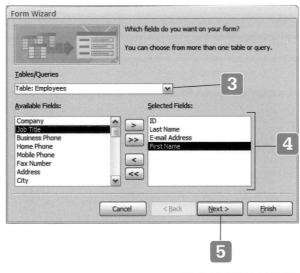

DID YOU KNOW?

Other buttons available on the Create tab let you create a blank form, a basic form or a split form, among others.

Create a form – part 2

After you get started with the fields for your form, you need to choose its design style and assign a name to it.

1 Choose the type of form you want.

2 Click Next.

3 Enter a name for the form.

4 Click Finish.

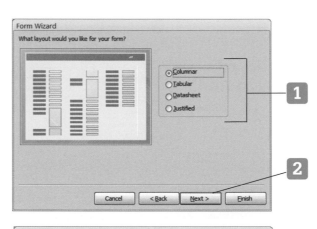

DID YOU KNOW?

The style of the form is important because it affects its formatting and final appearance. Look closely at the preview that appears on the left-hand side of the dialogue box.

Enter data in a form

Once you have created a form, you can add data to it.

1. Click the Forms button in the navigation bar.
2. Double-click the form to open it.
3. Type the data in the first field.
4. Press Tab to move to the next field and enter data in it.
5. When you are finished, click New Record to enter another record.

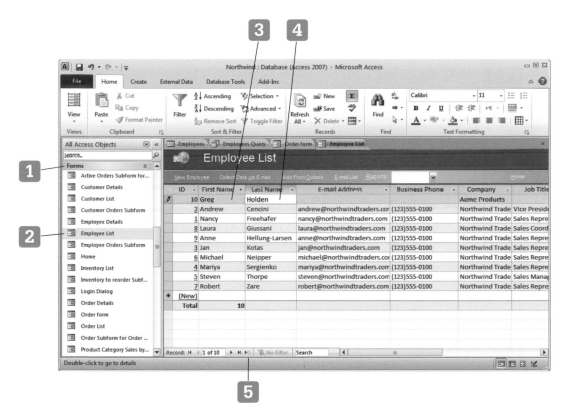

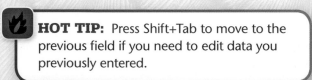

HOT TIP: Press Shift+Tab to move to the previous field if you need to edit data you previously entered.

Create a report

To produce a report with Access, you can use one of the form buttons on the Create tab. They let you create a basic report or blank report. You can also use the Report Wizard, which gives you a user-friendly way to select the information you want presented.

1 Click the Reports button in the navigation pane.

2 Click the table you want to use in the report.

3 Click the Create tab.

4 Click the Report Wizard button.

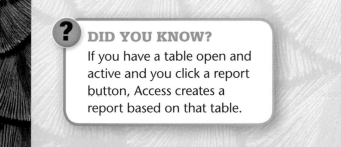

? DID YOU KNOW?

If you have a table open and active and you click a report button, Access creates a report based on that table.

5 Choose the table or query on which you want to base the form.

6 Choose the fields you want to include.

7 Click Next. In subsequent screens, you have the opportunity to specify any groupings of records and the order of records within each group. You can also choose the layout of the report, and its style.

8 Name your report and click Finish.

Change page setup

Once you create a report or form, it's a good idea to pay attention to the page set-up, which sets the margins, paper size, orientation, and grid and column settings.

1 Click the report, form, table or other object whose set-up you want to change in the navigation pane.

2 Click the File menu, click Print and click Print Preview.

3 Click the Margins button and choose Normal, Wide or Narrow.

4 Click Size and select the size you want.

5 Click Portrait or Landscape orientation.

6 Click Close Print Preview.

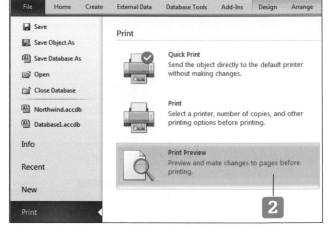

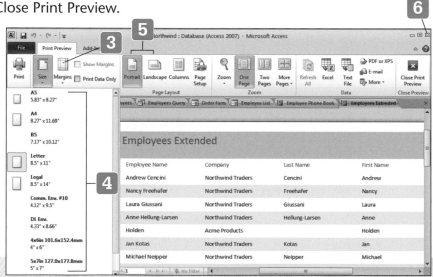

? DID YOU KNOW?

Portrait orients the page so it is taller than it is wide; landscape orients the page so it is wider than it is tall.

Back up a database

It's always important to back up your electronic data. Backups are especially important when you have spent considerable time compiling and formatting databases, and those databases are full of critical personal or business information. Access streamlines the process of backing up databases with a single command.

1 Save and close all your database objects.

2 Click the File tab.

3 Click Share, and click Back Up Database.

4 Click the Save in down arrow and select a location for the backup.

5 Change the backup name to something different than the original file name.

6 Click Save.

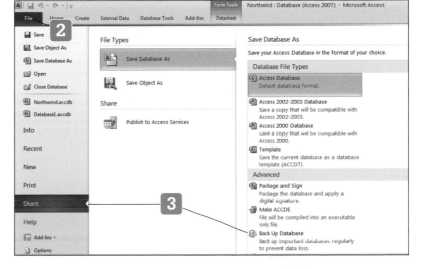

ALERT: Don't save your backup on the same computer or disk as the original. Save it on a removable disk or network drive so you have a copy in more than one location.

? DID YOU KNOW?
You can compact a database, including a backup, so that it takes up less disk space. Open the file, click Office, point to Manage and click Compact and Repair Database.

Publish a database online

SharePoint is a server environment that Microsoft provides to businesses and individuals to share files and other resources. If you have access to a server running SharePoint, you can quickly publish an access database to the server by following these steps:

1 Save and close all your database objects.

2 Click the File tab, then Share.

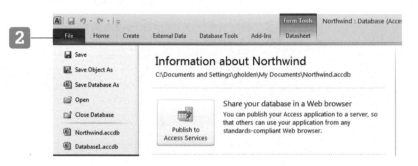

3 Enter the address of your SharePoint server.

4 Click Publish to Access Services.

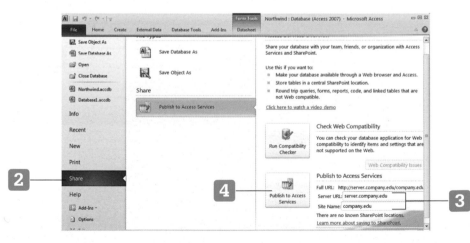

🔥 **HOT TIP:** You can find out more about SharePoint at http://sharepoint.microsoft.com.

9 Getting organised with Outlook

Introduction

The programs described in preceding chapters give you sophisticated ways to manage information. Another essential aspect of working with information is communication. In order to collaborate with friends and business colleagues, you need to be able to contact them and communicate the information you have gathered. Outlook 2010 gives you a user-friendly, yet powerful way to both organise events and contacts and reach the people with whom you need to connect.

Outlook helps you keep track of appointments and meetings with its calendar. It makes it easy to store contact information from addresses to phone numbers for all your friends, family members and business associates. Its Notes feature allows you to write reminders to yourself, and its Tasks feature gives you a place to assemble a to-do list. And it's a full featured email application as well.

This chapter's tasks will help you organise your day-to-day activities with features that are easy to use and easy to customise as well. You'll soon be up and running with the functions that let you accomplish all of your digital communication needs.

Start Outlook for the first time

The first time you start Outlook, you are given the opportunity to configure your personal profile. Don't skip these steps: they guide you through the information you need to send and receive email and set up contacts in address books.

Start Outlook by clicking the Start button, pointing to All Programs, clicking Microsoft Office and choosing Microsoft Office Outlook 2010.

2 When the Welcome screen appears, click Next.

3 In the next screen, when you are asked to configure an email account, click Yes.

4 Click Next.

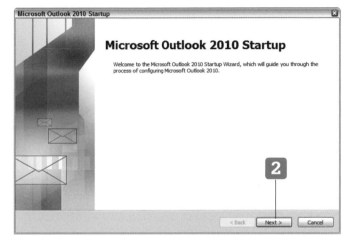

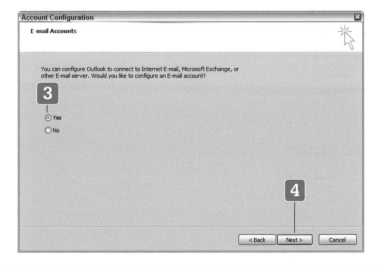

? DID YOU KNOW?

If you don't have your email account information ready, click No. You can add your account information later on.

? DID YOU KNOW?

You can configure Outlook to work with another email account at any time. Click Tools, click Account Settings, click the email tab, click Add and follow the instructions on the wizard that appears to help you set up the account.

5 Type your email account information.

6 Click Next. A dialogue box appears, giving you the progress of connecting to your email server.

Add New Account ☒

Auto Account Setup
Click Next to connect to the mail server and automatically configure your account settings.

⊙ **E-mail Account**

Your Name: `Greg Holden`
Example: Ellen Adams

E-mail Address: `gholden@netscape.net`
Example: ellen@contoso.com

5

Password: `********`
Retype Password: `********`
Type the password your Internet service provider has given you.

○ **Text Messaging**

6

○ **Manually configure server settings or additional server types**

< Back | Next > | Cancel

7 When the connection is established, click Finish.

Add New Account ☒

Online search for your server settings...

Configuring

Configuring e-mail server settings. This might take several minutes:
✓ Establish network connection
✓ Search for gholden@speakeasy.net server settings
✓ Log on to server and send a test e-mail message

Your **IMAP** e-mail account is successfully configured.

7

☐ Manually configure server settings | Add another account...

< Back | Finish | Cancel

ALERT: In order to make full use of Outlook's email, scheduling and contact capabilities, you need to be connected to the Internet or a local area network (LAN). A high-speed service such as a Digital Subscriber Line (DSL) or cable connection is optimal.

? DID YOU KNOW?
A profile is a set of information needed to access one or more address books or email accounts.

Customise your to-do list

One of the best ways to get started with Outlook is to preview your meetings, appointments and tasks for the day using the to-do bar, which appears on the right-hand side of the Outlook window. It gives you a convenient place to see all of the current day's events. The to-do bar has three view options: normal, minimised and off.

1 If the to-do bar is minimised, either single-click it or click the arrow at the top of the bar to expand it.

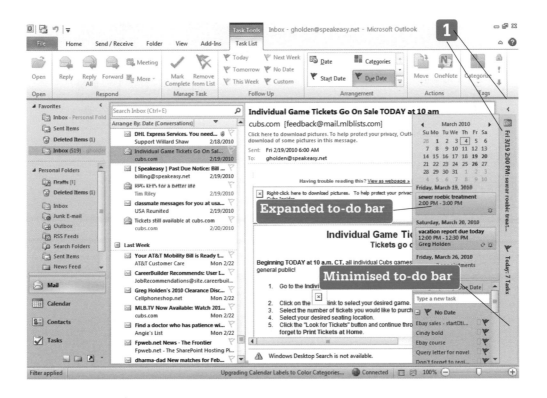

2 Click the View tab to customise the to-do bar's settings.

3 Click the To-Do Bar button.

4 Choose one of these options to change the appearance of the tab.

5 Tick items to show them; untick items to hide them.

6 Click Options for more control over to-do bar contents.

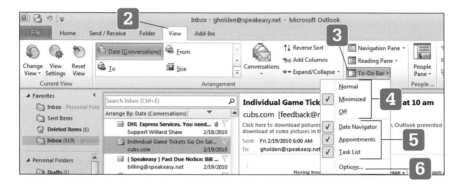

7 Untick items to hide them from the maximised to-do bar.

8 When you've finished customising your to-do bar, click OK.

! ALERT: In order to get a list of the day's events, you need to have recorded them beforehand. Get in the habit of recording events so you can track them as needed.

Add a task

In order to view tasks on your Outlook Today page, you need to have entered them beforehand. It only takes a few seconds to do so. You can add tasks for any date you wish as well.

1 Click the Tasks view bar.

2 Click the box that is initially labelled Type a new task and enter your own text. In the adjacent image, I have typed 'Pick up prescription.'

3 Press Enter.

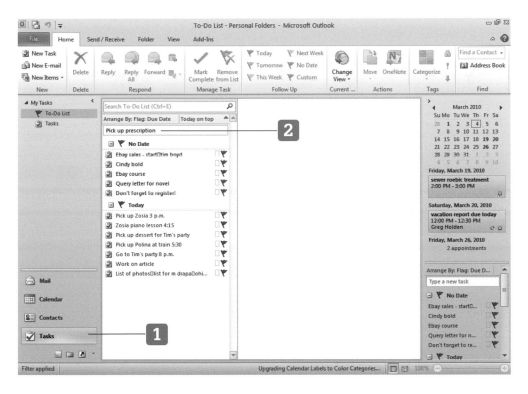

HOT TIP: To enter a task for a future date, select the data from the calendar at the top of the to-do bar. Use the left and right arrows to move back or forward one month, respectively.

Enter a calendar item

A calendar item is different than a task. The calendar can include appointments, meetings and other lists, not just tasks to do. You can enter not only the date of the event but the amount of time it will require from your schedule.

1 Click the Calendar view bar.

2 Choose the date.

3 Scroll down to the desired time.

4 Click the box next to the time, type the description and press Enter.

? DID YOU KNOW?

You can share your calendar with others on your network by clicking How to Share Calendars and following the instructions in the Help file that appears.

Navigate through your Outlook data

The navigation pane, which appears on the left-hand side of the Outlook window, lets you move and enter data and view your information in different ways. By default, the Mail, Calendar, Contacts and Tasks view buttons appear near the bottom of the pane. You can add more views by clicking the Configure buttons drop-down arrow.

1️⃣ Click a calendar date to view or enter tasks and other information for that date.

2️⃣ Click one of the view buttons at the bottom of the pane to view a particular type of data.

3️⃣ Click the Close button to close the navigation pane.

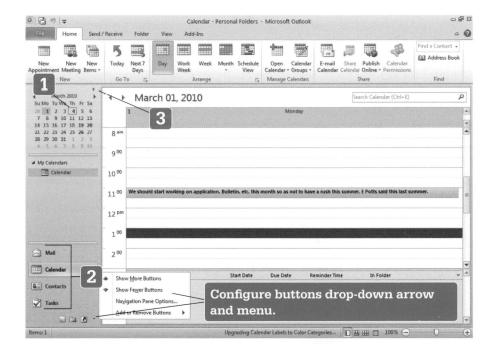

Configure buttons drop-down arrow and menu.

? DID YOU KNOW?

The double arrows in the upper right-hand corner of the navigation pane let you minimise or maximise the navigation pane. Click to minimise the pane when you need more room to work with information in the reading pane.

? DID YOU KNOW?

The Go menu gives you an alternative way to navigate through Outlook. It's a good alternative if you close the navigation pane to save space.

Customise the navigation pane

You might not know the full range of information that the Outlook pane can provide unless you customise the pane. You can add or remove the view buttons at the bottom of the pane or change their order as well.

1 Click the Configure Buttons drop-down arrow, point to Add or Remove Buttons and choose a button from the menu.

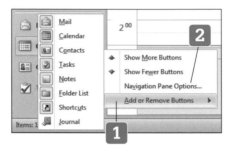

2 To change the order of buttons or add or remove buttons, click Configure Buttons and choose Navigation Pane Options.

3 To display a button, make sure the box next to it is ticked.

4 To remove a button, untick the box next to it.

5 To reorder a button, click it and then click Move Up or Move Down.

6 When you've finished, click OK.

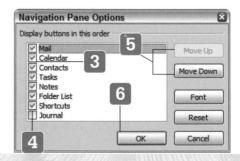

HOT TIP: Click Reset to restore the set of view buttons to their original state.

View items

Each of the views listed in the navigation pane (Mail, Calendar, Contacts, Tasks, and so on) have folders within them. Within each of those folders are stored the individual items that make up your Outlook data. You can then edit, delete or organise each item as needed.

1 Click one of the view buttons on the navigation pane to switch to the Outlook view you want. In the image shown here, Tasks view is chosen.

2 Click the Change View down arrow.

3 Choose a view you want to use.

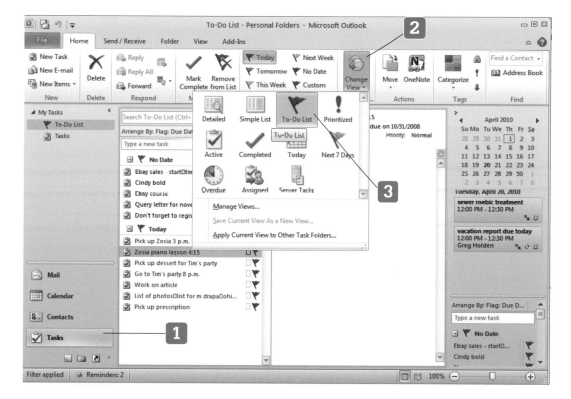

View folders

Each of your tasks, contacts, or other bits of information are stored within folders. You can view and edit the folders as you wish by choosing them in the navigation pane.

1 Click the Folder List icon at the bottom of the navigation pane.

2 Click a folder in the list to view its contents in the reading pane.

3 Right-click an item and choose New Folder from the context menu to create a new subfolder within the main folder.

HOT TIP: The Search Folders item at the bottom of the Folder List lets you search your email for different criteria. A search folder is a virtual folder that collects sets of criteria you might want to search regularly. By default, you have three search folders: Categorized Mail, Large Mail and Unread Mail. You can create a new search folder by clicking Mail View, clicking the File menu, pointing to New and clicking Search Folders. In the New Search Folder dialogue box, click any one of the predefined Search Folders and then customise it so it has the criteria you want.

Subscribe to an RSS feed

Outlook includes a reader for Really Simple Syndication (RSS) feeds that keep you updated with blogs, news feeds or other information on the Web. In order to receive a feed put out by a blog or website, you need to subscribe to it. You can do so either within Internet Explorer or Outlook. This task shows you how to subscribe using Outlook.

1 Right-click the RSS feed displayed on a webpage and click Copy link address from the context menu that appears.

2 Switch to Outlook and click the Folder List if necessary.

3 Right-click the RSS Feeds folder and choose Add a New RSS Feed from the context menu.

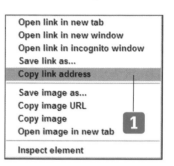

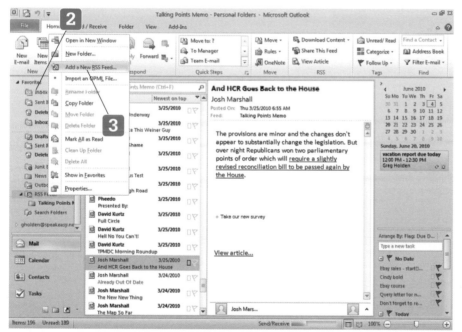

🔥 HOT TIP: Click the plus sign next to the RSS Feeds folder. You'll find that you are already subscribed to several feeds.

❓ DID YOU KNOW?

If you browse to a website that provides an RSS feed, you can click the RSS Feeds link and then click Subscribe to this feed. You can then read the feed using Outlook.

Add a new contact

Contacts are one of the fundamental pieces of information you can track and work with in Outlook. A contact is a person or business you need to communicate with, either by phone, fax, IM, text or email. Outlook can help you with all of these media: it gives you a way to store names, addresses and contact information, as well as other essential information about each contact such as birthdays, account information, company names or titles.

1 Click the Contacts view button in the navigation pane.

2 Click New Contact.

HOT TIP: Double-click anywhere in the reading pane to create a new contact.

3 When the Contact window opens, fill in the contact information.

The Contact window contains its own set of Home tab options.

4 When you enter a phone number, fill in your current location in the Location Information dialogue box and then click OK.

5 Click Details on the Contacts tab and fill in more detailed information about the contact.

6 Click the Save & Close button on the Contacts tab.

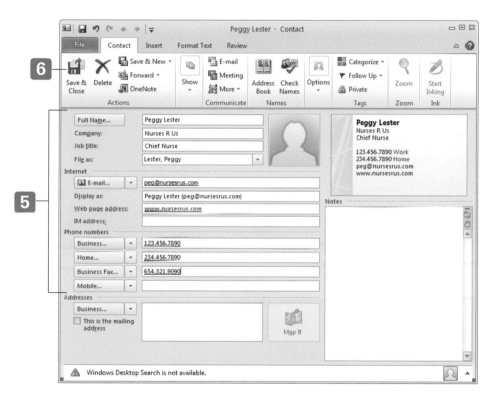

Display and edit a business card

An electronic business card (EBC) is the 'short version' of a contact. It is created in the process of assembling contact information. The EBC appears in the upper right-hand corner of the Contact window. It includes a name, job title, company name, phone number, and other basic contact details.

1. Click the Business Card button in the Current View group of the Home tab.

2. Double-click the contact you want to view.

3. Click Options and then click the Business Card button on the Contact tab.

4. Click the line of the business card you want to edit.

5. Make the changes you want.

6. Click OK.

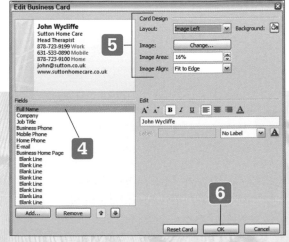

HOT TIP: Click Reset Card to remove any formatting changes you made so you are left with a generic card.

Create a contact group

A contact group is a set of contacts that you can treat as a single entity. It's similar to a mailing list in the world of email: you can send a single message or task request to the group as a whole. Instead of having to communicate with each list member individually, you can send a message to everyone at once.

1 Click the Contacts view button on the navigation pane.

2 Click the New Contact Group button on the Home tab. The Distribution List window opens.

3 Type a name for your Contact Group.

4 Click Add Members.

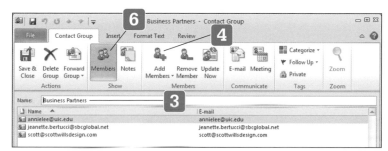

5 Select the names you want to add.

6 Click the Members button in the Show group. You will see your new list.

7 Click OK.

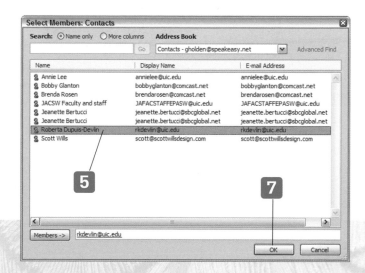

HOT TIP: Press Ctrl+Shift+L to quickly open the Distribution List window.

DID YOU KNOW? Click Add New to add a new name to the list.

Create and address an email message

One of Outlook's most basic functions is the ability to send and receive email messages. You do so in the Untitled Message window. Here you address the message, type the text, check over what you've typed, and send it.

1 Click the Mail button in the navigation pane.

2 Click the New E-mail button.

3 Enter the email address of the recipient you want, or click the To button and choose a recipient from your list of contacts.

4 Click Cc and choose any recipients who should receive a copy of the message.

5 Type the text of your message.

6 Click the Review tab and then click Spelling & Grammar to check the spelling of your text.

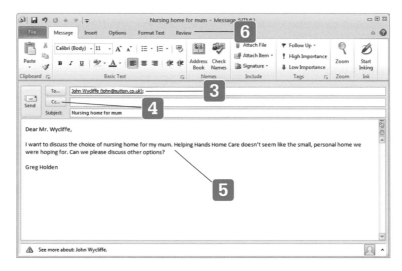

HOT TIP: You can send a message to multiple addresses by separating each recipient with a semicolon (;). Press Enter after each email address and the semicolon will be entered automatically.

Attach a file to an email message

An attachment is an image, text or other file you send along with the text of an email message. Because you're using Outlook 2010, you have the added advantage of being able to send an Outlook task, contact or note.

1 Once you have composed your email message text, click the Attach Item or Attach File icon in the Include group in the Message tab, which appears at the top of the Message window.

2 In the Insert File dialogue box, locate the file you want to attach.

3 Click Insert.

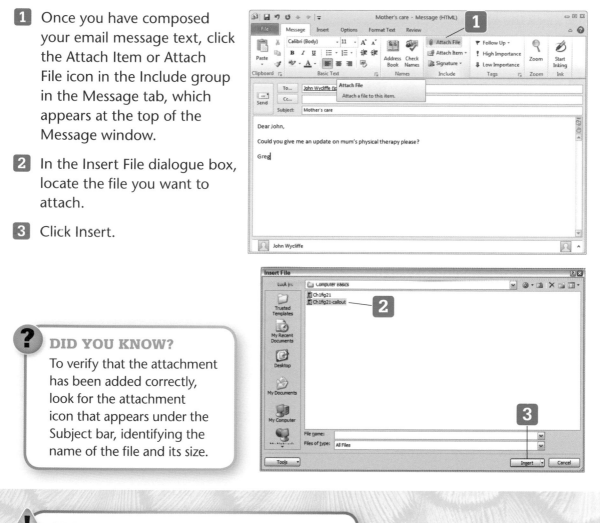

? DID YOU KNOW?

To verify that the attachment has been added correctly, look for the attachment icon that appears under the Subject bar, identifying the name of the file and its size.

! ALERT: Take care with the size of your attachments. Files over 1 MB in size (such as digital photos) not only take a long time to send, but they may be blocked by some email services. To send a large attachment, pack it in a file archive program such as WinZip (http://www.winzip.com).

Create a signature file

A signature file is a bit of text you can add to the end of all your email messages. Signature files can identify you and even help you market yourself and your business. You don't have to type a signature file every time you send a message; by saving the information you need in a text file, you can have Outlook add it automatically to the end of your messages.

1 Click the File tab, and then click Options.

2 When the Outlook Options dialogue box opens, click Mail.

3 Click Signatures.

4 Click New, type a name for your signature file and click OK.

5 Type your signature file text.

6 Click OK twice.

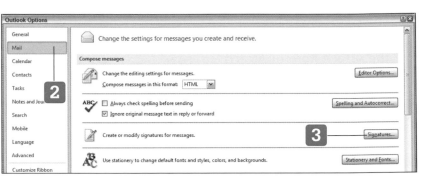

 DID YOU KNOW?

Be sure to type a short and easy-to-remember name for your signature file so you can find it easily. You can have more than one signature file and attach them to messages for different purposes.

DID YOU KNOW?

Use the formatting controls in the Signatures and Stationery dialogue box to give your signature file some graphic interest. Select the text you want to format and click the controls to make it bold or centred, or to add a hyperlink.

Send an email message

When you have typed the text of your email message and have attached files and signatures as needed, you can send it. You can send and receive messages at the same time, and control the way Outlook sends messages as well. When you send a message, Outlook moves it to the Outbox folder, where it stays while Outlook connects to your email server and sends the mail.

1 Create your message.

2 Click the Send button to send the file.

3 To change the way Outlook sends and receives email, click the Options tab and then click More Options.

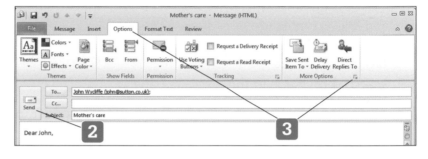

4 Click the down arrow next to Importance and choose the level of importance for the message.

5 Click here to have a delivery receipt sent to yourself.

6 Check this box and enter a time to schedule later delivery of the message.

7 Click OK.

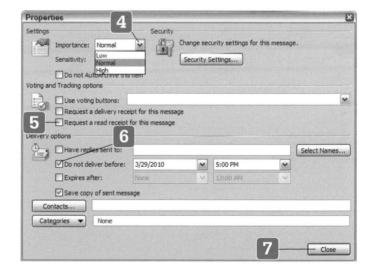

? **DID YOU KNOW?**

To insert a miniature version of your calendar in an email message, click the Insert tab at the top of the message window, and then click the Calendar button.

Read email messages

You don't necessarily have to do anything to have Outlook retrieve your email. As long as your computer is connected to the Internet and Outlook is open, the program will check for and receive your email at regular intervals. You can also click Send/Receive to have Outlook check your mail and retrieve any incoming messages at any time.

1 To check for incoming messages, click the Send/Receive tab, and then click Send/ Receive All Folders.

If a message arrives, you see an alert in the taskbar. An envelope icon appears to let you know a message is ready.

2 Click the message header in the Inbox to display the message.

3 Read the message in the message pane.

4 To open an attachment, double-click the file to open it, or:

- Right-click the attachment, click Save As, find a location and click OK.

- Click the attachment and then click Preview.

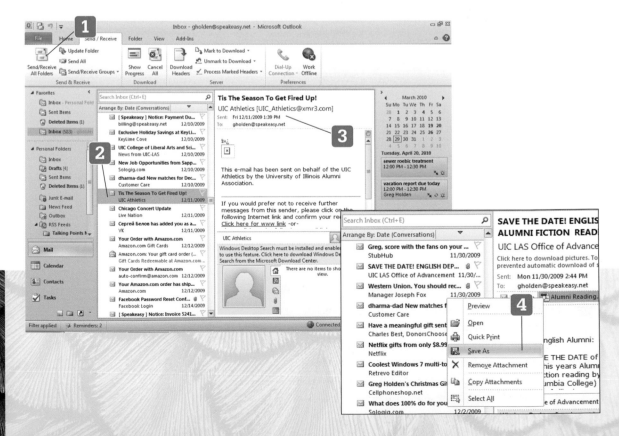

Search your email

If you have let your email pile up to hundreds or even thousands of messages, it can be a challenge to find a message from a particular individual or with a particular keyword in the subject line. Outlook, however, makes it easy for you to search for and locate the messages you want. Outlook 2010 adds a new feature: Windows Desktop Search, the ability to search through email in your inbox and on your computer as well.

1 Click the Mail view button.

2 Click once in the search box above the message list. The Search Tools tab appears.

3 If you want to search by date, or by whether messages were sent or received, click Search Tools and choose Advanced Find from the drop-down list.

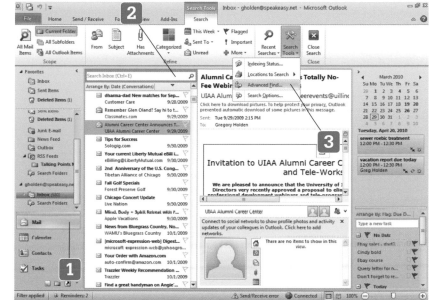

4 Enter criteria in the From, Sent To, Time or other boxes.

5 Click Find Now; the search results automatically appear beneath the Instant Search pane.

HOT TIP: If you currently have the Inbox open and choose to search email, you will only search through the messages in your Inbox. But you might want to search for messages you have sent. Click Sent Items to view your sent messages. Then open the Instant Search pane to search through these messages.

Top 10 Office 2010 Problems Solved

Problem 1: An Office program doesn't run properly. What can I do?

The first line of defence, if you find that an Office application isn't operating properly, is to use the Office Diagnostics application. This feature is available to all of Office's applications. Use it if you see an alert message or other indications that your Office program can't find data, is running slowly, or is experiencing mix-ups with data stored in the Windows registry.

1 Click Start.

2 Click Control Panel.

3 Click Programs.

4 Click Programs and Features.

5 Click the application you want to repair.

6 Click Change.

7 Click Repair and click Continue. The dialogue box notifies you of the progress of the repair.

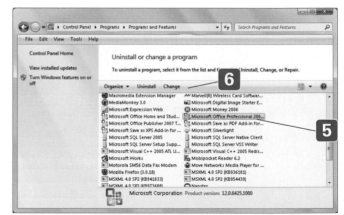

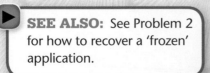

SEE ALSO: See Problem 2 for how to recover a 'frozen' application.

Problem 2: How do I recover a 'frozen' application?

Sometimes, applications 'freeze' (in other words, cease to respond to mouse clicks or other input) for one reason or another. Lack of computer memory or other problems can cause an application to be non-responsive. You don't have to completely restart your system in order to recover a non-responsive Office program, however. Follow these steps to use Microsoft Office Application Recovery.

1 Click Start, click All Programs, click Microsoft Office 2010, click Microsoft Office Tools and click Microsoft Office Application Recovery.

2 The Microsoft Office Application Recovery window opens with a list of currently open Office applications.

3 Click the application that is non-responsive and then click one or more of the maintenance buttons:

- Recover Application lets you restart the program if you want to keep working with it.

- End Application lets you close the application altogether.

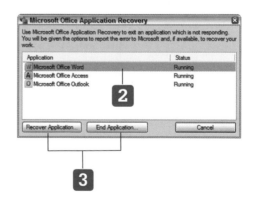

HOT TIP: The Windows Task Manager also lets you end a non-responsive application. Press Ctrl+Alt+Delete all together to open the Task Manager. Click the application that is non-responsive, and then click End Now to force the application to close.

Problem 3: I need to enable Safe Mode. What do I do?

You might be familiar with Safe Mode from problems with the Windows operating system: if the system encounters a serious problem, you have the option of starting in Safe Mode to repair it. Office 2010 also switches to Safe Mode when it encounters major difficulties.

In fact, Office uses two types of Safe Modes: Automated and User-Initiated. If an Office program is not able to start up after encountering problems, it automatically starts in Safe Mode the next time you try to use it. But you may need to manually enable Safe Mode yourself to make this option available.

1 Click the File tab and click Options.

2 Click Trust Center in the left-hand pane.

3 Click Trust Center Settings.

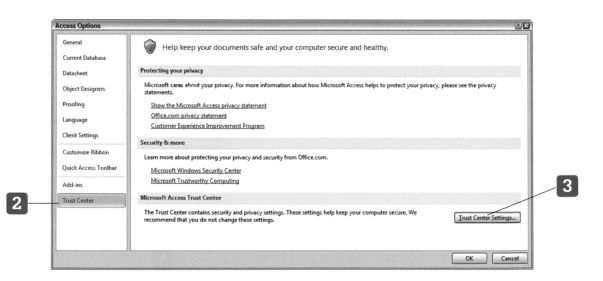

ALERT: When an Office program starts in Safe Mode, some of its features are unavailable. You can't save templates, for instance. Once you are in safe mode you can track which features are disabled in the Trust Center. You can enable them one at a time to pinpoint the problem.

4 Click ActiveX Settings.

5 Click the check box next to Safe Mode (helps limit the controls access to your computer).

6 Click OK here and in the next window to close it.

Problem 4: How do I start user-initiated Safe Mode?

If you encounter problems with one or more Office applications and that application does not go into Safe Mode automatically, you can start it up with user-initiated Safe Mode.

1 Click the Start button on the taskbar.

2 Click All Programs and double-click Microsoft Office.

3 Alternatively, point to the program you want to open if it is already in the Start menu.

4 Press and hold down the Ctrl key.

5 Click the program to open it in Safe Mode.

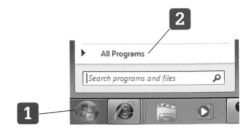

HOT TIP: You can also use the Run menu to start a program in user-initiated Safe Mode. Click the Start button, and type Run in the box at the bottom of the Start menu. Select Run, press Enter, and then start the program by adding the instruction 'safe' at the end of the command line.

Problem 5: How do I correct an Excel formula?

Formulas in Excel can quickly become complicated, but tools are available to help you track down problems. One, the Watch Window, keeps track of cells you specify. If you make changes to a worksheet that affect the cells and any formulas associated with them, the Watch Window lets you know about problems.

1 Open the worksheet you want to monitor, and select the cells you want to watch.

2 Click the Formulas tab.

3 Click Watch Window.

4 Click the Add Watch button in the Watch Window dialogue box.

5 Click Add.

6 Click Close.

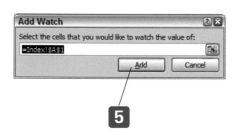

HOT TIP: To select all of a worksheet's cells at once, click the button in the upper left-hand corner, which simply has an arrow pointing down and to the right. Otherwise click and drag over cells to select them.

Problem 6: How do I check an Excel worksheet for errors?

The Error Checker is another automated feature that tracks any errors in your worksheet formulas. It follows rules that apply to formula preparation to uncover problems. The Error Checker works in the background while you edit your worksheet.

1 Open the worksheet you want to check for errors.

2 Click the Formulas tab.

3 Click the Error Checking button, and choose Error Checking from the drop-down list. The error checker automatically scans the worksheet for errors.

4 Click Resume if needed.

5 If an error is found, choose one of the buttons to handle the problem. For instance, click Trace Empty Cell to point to the cell that contains the problem.

6 Click Previous or Next to proceed with the check. When you've finished checking for errors, click Close.

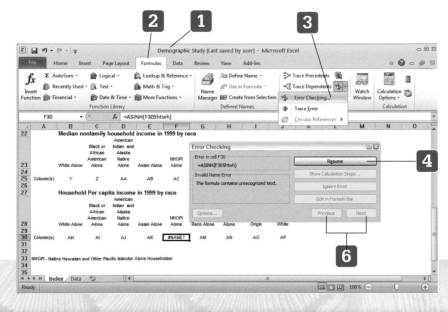

Problem 7: I think my Access database needs repairing. What do I do?

If you encounter problems with an Access 2010 database – for instance, if the program crashes when you try to gather data – it might mean the database has become corrupted or is too large. Access has a utility that can repair many of the problems that can cause databases to be corrupted.

1 Open the database you want to repair.

2 Click the File tab.

3 Click Compact & Repair database.

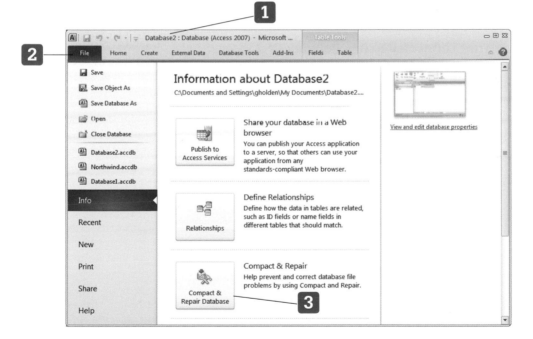

SEE ALSO: See Chapter 8 for more on maintaining databases, including compacting them to keep them at a manageable size.

Problem 8: I can't send or receive emails. What do I do?

It's not unusual to press Outlook's Send and Receive button only to discover that the program cannot perform this function. Usually, it means Outlook is unable to connect to your email server.

Before you call your Internet Service Provider's support staff, you should try a few debugging procedures on your own. Often, you can troubleshoot the problem yourself.

1 If you are connected to the Internet via an Ethernet cable, make sure the cable is plugged in securely both to your computer and your router.

2 Point to the network icon in the system tray. If you are attempting to retrieve email from a remote server rather than your company or organisation's network, you should see the message Access: Local and Internet. If you see the message Access: Local Only, you are not connected to the Internet.

3 If you are not connected to any network or you see the Local Only message, right-click the Network icon and choose Troubleshoot problems.

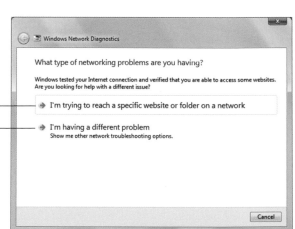

4 Wait for the network diagnostics tool to investigate the problem. Follow the recommendations in the diagnostics report.

HOT TIP: If you have Internet access but still can't retrieve email, use Outlook's repair feature to make sure your account information is correct. Click the File tab, click Account Settings, and choose Account Settings from the menu that appears. Choose the account you want to investigate and click Repair. Click Next and follow the steps shown in subsequent screens to repair the account information.

5 If you have a wireless connection, right-click the network icon and choose Connect to a network.

6 Choose your preferred network from the list and click Connect.

7 If you cannot connect, or if you connect but still don't have Internet access, restart your computer.

Problem 9: How do I repair a damaged document?

Sometimes, you try to open a file and things go wrong. The file either doesn't open, opens slowly, or doesn't open in its entirety. All Office programs have the ability to use a repair utility designed especially for damaged files.

1 Click the File tab and click Open to open the file you need to repair.

2 Click the Open down arrow.

3 Choose Open and Repair to open and repair the damaged file.

HOT TIP: You can also open the file from the list of recent documents, if it appears there.

Problem 10: How do I recover a damaged file?

Microsoft Word has a special utility that can help you recover text from a file that has been damaged. Use it if the option described in the previous section task fails to work.

1 Click the File tab and click Open.

2 Locate the file you need to repair.

3 Click the Files of type drop-down list.

4 Choose Recover Text from Any File.

5 When the Show Repairs dialogue box appears, click Close.

HOT TIP: You can also recover text from a damaged file using Open and Repair. Click File, click Open and select the file by single-clicking it. Then click the down arrow next to open and choose Open and Repair.

Use your computer with confidence

Office 2010	Excel 2010	Word 2010	Powerpoint 2010	Windows 7
9780273736127	9780273736134	9780273736141	9780273736158	9780273729136
Excel 2007	Office 2007	Laptop Basics Windows 7 Edition	Computer Basics Windows 7 edition	Windows Vista
9780273723547	9780273723554	9780273736806	9780273736844	9780273723493
Laptop Basics	Mac Basics	Computer Basics	Photoshop CS5	Photoshop Elements 8
9780273723486	9780273729297	9780273723479	9780273736820	9780273734390
Web Design	Netbook Basics	Windows 7 for the Over 50s	Laptop Basics for the Over 50s	Computer Basics for the Over 50s
9780273723530	9780273734925	9780273729181	9780273729129	9780273729174